PADDINGTON COLLEGE LIBRARY

036138

£7.99

KU-724-585

Annual Survey 2008

UK Government & Politics

Paul Fairclough
Richard Kelly
Eric Magee

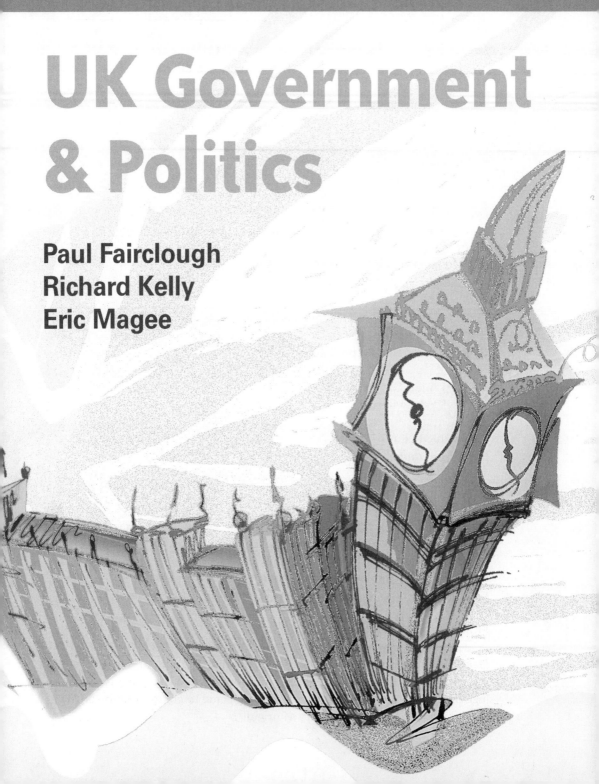

Philip Allan Updates, an imprint of Hodder Education, part of Hachette Livre UK, Market Place, Deddington, Oxfordshire OX15 0SE

Orders

Bookpoint Ltd, 130 Milton Park, Abingdon, Oxfordshire OX14 4SB
tel: 01235 827720
fax: 01235 400454
e-mail: uk.orders@bookpoint.co.uk

Lines are open 9.00 a.m.–5.00 p.m., Monday to Saturday, with a 24-hour message answering service. You can also order through the Philip Allan Updates website: www.philipallan.co.uk

© Philip Allan Updates 2008
ISBN 978-1-84489-702-5

First printed 2008
Impression number   5   4   3   2   1
Year   2013   2012   2011   2010   2009   2008

All rights reserved; no part of this publication may be reproduced, stored in a retrieval system, or transmitted, in any form or by any means, electronic, mechanical, photocopying, recording or otherwise without either the prior written permission of Philip Allan Updates or a licence permitting restricted copying in the United Kingdom issued by the Copyright Licensing Agency Ltd, Saffron House, 6–10 Kirby Street, London EC1N 8TS.

Printed by MPG Books, Bodmin

Hachette Livre UK's policy is to use papers that are natural, renewable and recyclable products and made from wood grown in sustainable forests. The logging and manufacturing processes are expected to conform to the environmental regulations of the country of origin.

P01171

Contents

CITY OF WESTMINSTER COLLEGE
LEARNING RESOURCE CENTRE
Date: 24.04.15
Acc. No. 036138
Class No. 320.941 FAI

Chapter 1

Blair to Brown: continuity or change?

About this chapter

Gordon Brown's 'coronation' as Labour leader and prime minister in the summer of 2007 marked the end of one of the longest-running sagas in modern UK politics. As noted in *Annual Survey 2007*, the Blair–Brown double act is said to have dated from the 1994 Granita pact where the two men supposedly met at the London restaurant in order to carve up the Labour leadership between themselves. It was agreed that Blair would take the top job. Brown would be chancellor of the exchequer, with the lure of significant influence over other departmental areas and a promise that he would become the prime minister during New Labour's second (ultimately its third) term in office.

This chapter examines the extent to which the new prime minister, Brown, was able to impose his own identity on a government that had been led by Blair for over a decade. It addresses questions such as:

■ Did Brown's first cabinet represent a clear break from what had gone before?
■ Was he able to impose his own style on the administration?
■ Was he able to establish a distinctive agenda on the domestic policy front?
■ Did his accession mark a sea change in the UK's relations with the European Union and with the USA?

Did Brown's first cabinet represent a clear break from what had gone before?

One of the first tasks to face the incoming prime minister was that of deciding just how many of the old guard should retain their positions in cabinet. There were significant winners and losers in a reshuffle (see Box 1.1) that was long anticipated, widely reported and — on the whole — well received.

Still out in the cold?

As expected, there was no return to cabinet for some of those former ministers most closely associated with Tony Blair: David Blunkett, Charles Clarke and Alan Milburn all remained on the backbenches. A return for either Milburn or Clarke would have been particularly surprising in light of the fact that both men had appeared to be trying to organise an 'anyone-but-Brown' campaign in the Labour leadership contest that had followed Blair's resignation.

Box 1.1 Brown's first cabinet

1	Gordon Brown	Prime Minister
2	Alistair Darling	Chancellor of the Exchequer
3	David Miliband	Secretary for Foreign and Commonwealth Affairs
4	Jack Straw	Secretary for Justice and Lord Chancellor
5	Jacqui Smith	Secretary for the Home Department
6	Des Browne	Secretary for Defence, and Secretary for Scotland
7	Alan Johnson	Secretary for Health
8	Hilary Benn	Secretary for Environment, Food and Rural Affairs
9	Douglas Alexander	Secretary for International Development
10	John Hutton	Secretary for Business, Enterprise and Regulatory Reform
11	Harriet Harman	Leader of the Commons, Minister for Women and Labour Party chair
12	Peter Hain	Secretary for Work and Pensions, and Secretary for Wales
13	Ed Miliband	Secretary for the Cabinet Office and Chancellor of the Duchy of Lancaster
14	Hazel Blears	Secretary for Communities and Local Government
15	Ruth Kelly	Secretary for Transport
16	Geoff Hoon	Chief whip
17	Ed Balls	Secretary for Children, Schools and Families
18	James Purnell	Secretary for Culture, Media and Sport
19	Shaun Woodward	Secretary for Northern Ireland
20	Lady Ashton	Leader of the Lords
21	Andy Burnham	Chief Secretary to the Treasury
22	John Denham	Secretary for Innovation, Universities and Skills

Note: also attending cabinet meetings: Tessa Jowell (Minister for the Olympics and Minister for London), Lord Grocott (Chief Whip of the Lords), Lady Scotland (Attorney General), Yvette Cooper (Minister for Housing); Mark Malloch Brown (Minister for Africa, Asia and the UN) and Beverley Hughes (Minister for Children, Young People and Families) who will attend negotiations on social policy.

Source: *Guardian*, 29 June 2007.

Off to pastures new?

Brown's first cabinet saw significant departures. Some left of their own volition: Patricia Hewitt (to spend more time with her ill mother); Lady Amos (to become EU representative to the African Union); Hilary Armstrong and John Reid, who both opted to leave office at the same time as Blair. Other long-serving cabinet members were overlooked; of these, Margaret Beckett was probably the most notable absentee. Beckett had served under Wilson and Callaghan in the 1970s, before becoming deputy party leader under John Smith in 1992 and the first female Labour Party leader in 1994 (albeit only briefly, following John Smith's sudden death). Latterly, Beckett achieved another female first when she was appointed to the post of foreign secretary. It was criticism of her performance in this role that made her vulnerable in Brown's reshuffle and it was no surprise, therefore, that she became the fourth senior female cabinet member not to survive the handover of power from Blair to Brown.

The onward and upward march of the new guard?

The reshuffle saw a significant number of highly regarded, although younger and less experienced, individuals assume senior positions in the government. Three of the six former special advisors identified in *Annual Survey 2006* as having been fast-tracked for high office found themselves in Brown's first cabinet (see Table 1.1). Ed Balls took the post of Secretary for Children, Schools and Families, following the reorganisation of the Department for Education and Skills; his wife Yvette Cooper was granted the right to attend cabinet meetings as Minister for Housing. The cabinet also included brothers Ed and David Miliband, who took on the Cabinet Office and the Foreign Office portfolios respectively. The latter's selection was particularly significant given the older Miliband's widely reported reservations regarding the military interventions in Afghanistan and Iraq.

Name	Constituency	Ranking in list of safe Labour seats*
David Miliband	South Shields	38
Ed Miliband	Doncaster North	41
Pat McFadden	Wolverhampton South East	58
Ed Balls	Normanton	121
Kitty Ussher	Burnley	223
Ian Austin	Dudley North	241

* Ranked by % majority in 2005.

Table 1.1 'Spinning' into the Commons

The Home Office/Justice Ministry split announced before Brown took on the top job (see 'What's new', *Politics Review*, Vol. 17, No. 2) paved the way for the departure of Lord Falconer. The assimilation of his Department of Constitutional Affairs into the new Justice Ministry had made it increasingly untenable for an unelected member to hold the post. Following the reshuffle, Jack Straw took on the role of Minister for Justice and Lord Chancellor. At the same time, Jacqui Smith became the first female home secretary and — at 44 — the second youngest ever to hold the post (Winston Churchill took on the role aged 35). Smith, elected to the Commons for the first time in 1997, had been one of the so-called 'Blair's babes' photographed with the then prime minister outside Parliament.

A government of all the talents?

The run-up to the announcement of Brown's first cabinet saw a good deal of coverage regarding the prime minister's oft-stated desire to create a 'government of all the talents' (see Box 1.2).

Box 1.2 Government of all the talents?

Mr Brown yesterday recruited a former sea lord, a surgeon, a rabbi, a QC, a former director general of the CBI and a Scotland Yard commissioner to join his first government. At least three Liberal Democrats will also act as advisors to Mr Brown.

Mr Brown's effort to recruit from outside Labour ranks — he repeatedly said that he wanted a government of all the talents — is designed to neutralise criticism that he is a Labour tribalist, and mirrors the efforts of Nicolas Sarkozy in France to look for ministers beyond his own party.

Source: adapted from Patrick Wintour, 'Brown parades his show of talent', *Guardian*, 30 June 2007.

In the days immediately before the first appointments were formally announced, speculation grew that Brown might even offer cabinet positions to senior Liberal Democrats, such as Lady Julia Neuberger, Dame Shirley Williams and the former Liberal Democrat leader, Lord Ashdown (the latter being widely tipped for the post of Northern Ireland secretary).

Some saw such a move as blatant politicking on the part of Brown — an effort to further undermine the Liberal Democrats and their then leader Menzies Campbell. However, those approached by the prime minister appeared to view the contact as genuine enough. Although the efforts to recruit Liberal Democrats to cabinet posts ended following the intervention of the Liberal Democrat leader, the possibility of some senior Liberal Democrats offering advice to the government on a more informal basis remained. On 20 June, the *Guardian* reported that both Lord Lester and Lady Julia Neuberger would advise the government while remaining Liberal Democrats, and Lady Williams — one of the original 'Gang of Four' who had left Labour in 1981 in order to form the SDP — might also take on a role advising the government in the area of nuclear non-proliferation. Although senior Liberal Democrats did not, in the end, take up ministerial positions, a number of 'Westminster outsiders' were drafted in to fill government posts.

Brown's willingness to look beyond the ranks of his parliamentary party was initially well received in the media, but had become a distraction by the end of 2007. On 18 November, the *News of the World* ran a damning exclusive on the government's efforts to get GMTV presenter Fiona Phillips to swap her breakfast television sofa for an office in the Department of Health (see Box 1.3) — a story also picked up by the *Guardian* a day later. Even the political editor of Britain's biggest selling Sunday tabloid appeared incredulous that Ms Phillips could find herself presiding over the licensing of new drugs. What next, the paper suggested: Jeremy Clarkson as transport minister; or Jerry Springer at the Department of Justice?

Box 1.3   Baroness Fiona Phillips?

Gordon Brown offered GMTV host Fiona Phillips a job as MINISTER in the government. The PM made the astonishing approach in the summer as he tried to poach people to form his 'government of all the talents'.

Mr Brown told the breakfast sofa chat queen she was 'a great communicator' and offered to fast-track her into government. Fiona, 46, would have been given a seat in the House of Lords, becoming BARONESS PHILLIPS.

[As] a Minister of State in the Department of Health...Fiona would have been tackling issues like obesity, smoking, abortion, sexual health and IVF. She would also have been in charge of licensing new drugs and funding cutting-edge medical research.

But the telly favourite turned the job down because she would have been forced to take a whopping £400,000-a-year pay cut.

Source: adapted from Ian Kirby, 'Chat queen to minister', *News of the World*, 18 November 2007.

Was the new prime minister able to impose his own style on the administration?

Style was always likely to be an issue for the incoming prime minister. Though Blair ultimately lost the confidence of many of his colleagues and the public at large — particularly in the wake of the Iraq intervention — one should not forget the extent to which his style and force of personality had driven the party on between 1994 and 2005. Even at the supposedly 'bitter end', Blair was held in high public regard. For example, faced with the question, 'Do you think that Tony Blair has been a good or bad prime minister?' in the Communicate Research poll on 1 May 2007 (published in the *Independent*), 61% responded 'good', with only 36% opting for 'bad'.

In contrast to his predecessor at No. 10, Brown had often been seen as cold and distant during his time as chancellor; effective in post, but rather dour. Some had gone further still: in March 2007, senior civil servants in the Treasury had criticised his 'Stalinist' tendencies (see Box 1.4).

Box 1.4   Commissar Brown?

Labour MPs yesterday rallied to the defence of Gordon Brown in the face of unprecedented attacks on his leadership style by senior civil servants, including damning claims that Mr Brown behaves with Stalinist ruthlessness.

Lord Turnbull, the former Treasury permanent secretary alongside Mr Brown for 4 years and subsequently head of the civil service, claimed Mr Brown treated his colleagues with almost complete contempt.

Source: adapted from the *Guardian*, 21 March 2007.

Although his marriage, fatherhood and the way in which he had dealt with the loss of a child had shown the chancellor in a new light, it was widely felt that the prime minister elect still needed to show a little more warmth.

Brown clearly made a real effort to smile more and put more feeling into speeches during his early public engagements as prime minister. However, it is fair to say that he will never be 'the great communicator'. Brown's speech at the Labour Party conference in September was, as *The Economist* put it on 10 November, 'solid but unspectacular'. His first appearance in the hot seat at prime minister's questions was similarly faltering, with even the struggling Liberal Democrat leader Menzies Campbell able to get a laugh at the prime minister's expense.

New prime minister, new spin?

The extent to which Brown is able to manage his image and present himself in a more sympathetic light in the coming months will depend, in large part, on those senior advisors put in place at the time of his accession. The public perception of Blair was certainly shaped by the work of individuals such as Alastair Campbell during his early years in the post and it is likely that Brown's new team (see Box 1.5) will perform a similarly important role in moulding and marketing Blair's successor.

Box 1.5	The prime minister's new team
Tom Scholar	Chief of Staff and Principal Private Secretary to the Prime Minister
Michael Ellam	Director of Communications and PM's spokesman
Gavin Kelly	Deputy Chief of Staff
Spencer Livermore	Director of Political Strategy
Sue Nye	Director of Government Relations
Dan Corry	Head of Policy Unit
Damian McBride	Advisor to the government on political press issues
Jeremy Heywood	Head of Domestic Policy and Strategy
Jon Cunliffe	Head of International Economic Affairs, Europe and G8 sherpa
Simon McDonald	Head of Foreign and Defence Policy

Source: adapted from the *Guardian*, 28 June 2007.

Was Brown able to establish a distinctive agenda on the domestic policy front?

There was certainly no public expectation that the change in prime minister would have a significant impact on either the direction of government policy or the fortunes of the Labour Party. In an ICM poll for the *Guardian* (23 June 2007), 61% of voters thought that the performance of the government would remain about the same, and 49% of all voters thought that Labour under Brown would be less likely to win the next general election than Labour under Blair (with only 43% taking the opposite view).

In the media, some were rather more optimistic. Mary Riddell offered 'three cheers for this new bill of rights' (*Guardian*, 13 May 2007), claiming that 'one of the first plans of the prime minister-in-waiting is to create a written constitution', and that 'his real target may be the monarchy'. In the event, the publication of the *Governance of Britain* Green Paper in July 2007 (see Chapter 8) did not go nearly as far as Riddell had anticipated and many had hoped.

Notwithstanding these criticisms, Brown did make a number of significant pledges during his early weeks in office. Indeed, on 14 September, the *Guardian* reported that the new prime minister had made promises totalling £39 billion of new spending during his first 7 weeks in post. This total included:

- an extra £7.7 billion for defence, to 2011
- £15 billion to improve the railways
- £4 billion extra on early years education over 3 years
- £8 billion on affordable housing

Aside from precise pledges on government spending, there has also been the sense that Brown is more concerned with the issue of 'social mobility' than his predecessor; that much was made clear during his time as chancellor. The first Queen's Speech under Brown also suggested some significant departures from the Blairite agenda (see Box 1.6).

Box 1.6   Highlights from the Queen's Speech

- A new counter-terrorism bill that could extend the period of detention without charge, and a citizenship and immigration bill that would set out the rights and duties of citizens.

- A planning reform bill that would allow for the more speedy approval of major projects.

- A climate change bill that would make Britain the first country in the world to set legally binding limits on the emission of greenhouse gases.

- Further reform of party funding.

- The Commons to be given a consultative role ahead of any future deployment of troops into armed conflict.

- An employment bill that would impose tougher penalties on employers who fail to offer the minimum wage.

- Extension of the right to request flexible working to parents of school-age children.

- Reform on human fertilisation, protecting prospective parents from excessive charges, and relaxing restrictions on gay couples seeking such treatment, 'saviour siblings' and embryo research.

- The establishment of a single inspectorate — the Quality Care Commission — to regulate the NHS, private clinics, social care services and mental health establishments; easier prosecutions of failing doctors.
- An education and skills bill that could raise the school-leaving age to 18 from 2015; fines for students who fail to attend a course and for parents who actively prevent their children from attending school.

Source: drawn from 'Brown's first brings rights, duties and disappointment', *Guardian*, 7 November 2007.

Did Brown's accession mark a clear watershed in the UK's relations with the European Union and the USA?

During his time as chancellor, Gordon Brown gained a reputation as being unwilling to take full advantage of the opportunities for international diplomacy afforded him by virtue of his position. Stories abound of Brown sitting in Council of Ministers' meetings apparently paying little attention to, and having scant regard for, the needs of his European counterparts. Such a track record did little to suggest that the new prime minister would be seeking the kind of international profile so obviously coveted by his predecessor.

The reality, however, was that the international climate at the time of Brown's accession, not least the ongoing terrorist threat, made diplomatic isolationism a non-starter. If nothing else, Brown would surely have been mindful of the fact that when asked about Blair's legacy in a Communicate Research poll in the *Independent* (1 May 2007), the majority of respondents thought that Brown's predecessor would be remembered not for improving public services (only 2% of those questioned) or introducing the minimum wage (3%), but for taking the UK to war in Iraq (69%). Indeed, when one adds this figure to those who would remember Blair most for his contribution to the Northern Ireland peace process (6%) or his relationship with George W. Bush (9%), the picture was even more stark: diplomacy clearly matters.

So it was that in the early months of Brown's premiership he adopted a more internationalist approach — building bridges with his European partners, while also looking to maintain the special relationship with the USA, and keeping in mind the UK's commitments to the UN, the Commonwealth and NATO. On the European front, Brown was a major player in negotiations over the 2007 EU Reform Treaty (the 'Lisbon Treaty'), despite having been effectively dealt his hand in the negotiations by what Blair had agreed at the previous summit.

As regards UK relations with the USA, it is clear that the Brown–Bush axis is not nearly as strong as the understanding between Blair and Bush — a friendship that had, according to the President, been forged in war. Although Brown travelled to the USA in an effort to shore up the special relationship (see Box 1.7), his efforts were not entirely convincing; his appointment of war-sceptic David Miliband as foreign secretary had set the tone early on.

> **Box 1.7** **A (not so) special relationship?**
>
> Gordon Brown will seek to reassure the United States tonight that the special relationship still lies at the heart of British foreign policy, following concerns that transatlantic ties have been weakened since his predecessor departed.
>
> 'He is emphasising how important our relationship with the US is, to ensure that there are no misunderstandings there,' said a No. 10 source.
>
> Mr Brown's first visit to Washington as prime minister was over-shadowed by the foreign minister Lord Malloch-Brown's suggestion that Britain and the UK would no longer be 'joined at the hip'.
>
> Source: adapted from the *Guardian*, 12 November 2007.

None of this should be that surprising. The closeness of Blair's relationship with Bush was — as we have seen — a significant factor in the then prime minister's declining public standing. There would be little advantage to be had in Mr Brown tying himself to a US administration that is certain to end on 20 January 2009 and whose titular head, George W. Bush, is fast becoming the lamest of all lame ducks. For his part, President Bush spent the autumn of 2007 looking to develop closer relations with France and Germany through meetings with the French president Nicolas Sarkozy and the German chancellor Angela Merkel.

Conclusions

It is clearly far too early to judge just how effective a prime minister Gordon Brown may eventually become. What is clear, however, is that 10 years spent as chancellor — shielded from the full glare of media attention by a prime minister who revelled in it — has afforded the former chancellor little opportunity to develop the full range of skills he will need to succeed in the top job. Although the thoroughness and determination Brown demonstrated when chancellor have afforded him a certain amount of political capital, modern political leadership requires a clearer and more compelling vision than the prime minister has, as yet, been able to articulate (see Box 1.8).

> **Box 1.8** **The 'vision thing'**
>
> A pamphlet released on 1 November 2007 by the Fabian Society, a think-tank loyal to Mr Brown, urged him to do more of the 'vision thing'...
>
> Mr Brown is not entirely without a vision, though his opponents are right that he has not yet given it adequate expression. He is genuinely passionate about certain causes, and his legislative agenda suggests them. He plainly cares about social mobility, perhaps more than any other issue. And he has a long-standing, if guarded, interest in constitutional reform, an issue that seldom animated his predecessor. If he does not call an election until 2010...he will have other opportunities to sell these causes in a more exhilarating form. There is a story called Brownism, though it is one waiting to be told.
>
> Source: adapted from *The Economist*, 10 November 2007.

Summary

- The 'coronation' of Gordon Brown as prime minister brought significant changes in the composition of the cabinet.
- Although the Blair–Brown switch saw the departure of a number of senior female cabinet members, notably Margaret Beckett, there was also an influx of youth.
- Gordon Brown's efforts to create a 'government of all the talents' — though regarded as genuine by many commentators — met with only limited success.
- *The Governance of Britain* Green Paper (July 2007) and the Queen's Speech that followed in the autumn of 2007 offered a number of interesting initiatives on the domestic front, but those who had expected Brown to move towards a new codified constitution and bill of rights for the UK were left disappointed.
- In the area of foreign policy, Brown placed less emphasis on the special relationship with the USA, instead looking to organisations such as the UN and the EU.
- By the end of 2007, some were questioning whether the prime minister had the vision necessary to take the New Labour project forward.

Chapter 2

The 2007 elections: which parties prospered?

About this chapter

This chapter reviews the various elections held in 2007 and assesses their implications for the UK's main parties. It addresses questions such as:

- Did the Conservative Party's electoral revival stall?
- Is Labour's reputation as a 'dominant' party under threat?
- Have the Liberal Democrats faltered?
- How important are parties other than 'the big three'?
- Is there still such a thing as a 'British party system'?

Which elections took place in 2007?

For students of the UK party system, the key elections of 2007 were:

- The English and Scottish council elections (including mayoral elections in England) on 3 May.
- The Scottish Parliament elections on 3 May.
- The Welsh Assembly elections on 3 May.
- The parliamentary by-elections in Ealing Southall and Sedgefield on 19 July.
- The Northern Ireland Assembly elections on 7 March.

The council/mayoral elections

Elections were held in 312 English councils where, in most cases, a third of seats were contested. There were also mayoral elections in Bradford, Mansfield and Middlesborough. In Scotland, all seats were contested on all 32 councils. For the first time, Scottish councils were elected under the single transferable vote method of proportional representation. The results of the local government elections in England are shown in Table 2.1.

Party	Results		
	Councils won	Councillors elected	Share of votes cast (%)
Conservative	165 (+39)	5,458 (+927)	40
Labour	36 (−16)	2,225 (−642)	26
Liberal Democrat	23 (−5)	2,337 (−257)	24
Others	8 (−4)	1,678 (−30)	10

Turnout: 38%
Figures in brackets denote change since 2003

	Effects	
Party	Councils controlled	Council seats held
Conservative	206 (47%)	9,432 (43%)
Labour	58 (13%)	5,463 (25%)
Liberal Democrat	29 (7%)	4,406 (20%)
Others	13 (3%)	2,518 (12%)

There are 134 councils (30%) where no party has overall control

Table 2.1 English local government elections, 2007

Assessing the local elections: a Tory triumph?

After the local elections, Conservative officials cited plenty of reasons to be cheerful:

- The Tories won 40% of votes cast and had a 14% vote lead over Labour — figures consistent with a Tory majority at the next general election.
- The Tories made net gains of 39 councils and 927 seats. Indeed, they won no fewer than 47% of the seats contested — far more than commentators had predicted — and now hold 43% of council seats in Britain while controlling 53% of English councils.
- The Tories gained control of both Labour-held councils (e.g. Lincoln) and Liberal Democrat-held councils (e.g. Bournemouth).
- The Tories gained councils in all parts of England, for example Blackpool and Chester in the north, Rugby and Warwick in the Midlands, Dover and Dartford in the southeast, Plymouth and Torbay in the southwest.

All this suggested that, following their rejuvenation under David Cameron, the Tories were fast becoming the dominant political force, again enjoying the nationwide support needed to govern the country. However, there were some sobering facts for them to remember:

- Their claim to be a national party was undermined by their performance in Scotland, where they gained just 16 of the 148 seats lost by Labour and the Liberal Democrats. In addition, they still control no Scottish councils. Had it not been for proportional representation, the Tories in Scotland would have struggled to make any progress at all.
- Their claims of national revival were also weakened by a poor performance in the metropolitan areas of northern England: they still have no councillors in Manchester, Liverpool and Newcastle. Electoral history shows that, when it has no base in an area's council, a party struggles to mount an effective campaign in those areas at a general election.
- When Labour was in opposition in the mid-1990s — and poised to win a general election — its performance in local elections was much more dominant than the Tories' in 2007. In the 1995 local elections, for example, Labour won 47% of votes cast and had a 22% lead over John Major's Tories. Furthermore, the Tories' vote share in 2007 was only 2% higher than at the

local elections of 2000, just a year before they crashed to another general election defeat.

Assessing the local elections: unmitigated disaster for Labour?

With much public disquiet over government policy (notably in respect of Iraq and public service reform), plus intra-party tensions caused by Blair's imminent departure, Labour was braced for bad results. There was certainly no shortage of setbacks for the governing party:

- At 26%, its national vote share was almost as bad as that suffered by the Tories in the mid-1990s, shortly before annihilation at the 1997 general election.
- Labour lost 505 seats in England and a further 137 in Scotland.
- As a result, the party is a much-diminished force in local government. Labour now controls only 12% of English councils and is without representation on 95 councils in England and Scotland. There are now fewer Labour councillors than at any time since 1974.

Amazingly, Labour ministers still managed to sound upbeat in the wake of the results, claiming they 'could have been worse' and pointing to a number of 'encouraging' factors:

- Despite what had been, by common consent, an exceptionally troubling year for Labour, its vote share was no lower than it had been in the local elections of 2004 — a year before the government was re-elected.
- In certain parts of the country, Labour more than held its own. Indeed, it took North Lincolnshire from the Tories and gained a majority in Leicester and Luton (previously hung).

As such, Labour was able to dismiss the 2007 results as just the latest example of governing parties suffering severe loss of support in council elections — support that history suggests can be reclaimed at a general election.

Assessing the local elections: Liberal Democrats floundering?

Traditionally, council elections are a chance for Britain's third party to shine, attracting substantial numbers of protest votes from those dissatisfied with the two main parties. There was much less evidence of this in the 2007 elections:

- Liberal Democrats suffered a net loss of 257 seats.
- They were left with no representation on 42 councils.
- They lost control of 11 councils, for example York and St Albans.
- They lost to the Tories a number of 'weather vane' southern councils, such as Torbay and Bournemouth, suggesting that Cameron's liberal Toryism was appealing to the centrist voters courted by Liberal Democrats.

However, leading Liberal Democrats claimed there was no cause for panic:

- They still control 23 councils and only have 5% fewer councillors than Labour.
- They gained control of Eastbourne and Hinckley/Bosworth from the Tories, and a further four previously hung councils.

- Their vote share of 24% was higher than in some of the local elections that took place when Charles Kennedy had been leader.

Nonetheless, these results did nothing to allay Liberal Democrat anxieties about the post-Kennedy party and fuelled doubts about the effectiveness of Menzies Campbell's leadership.

Assessing the local elections: multi-dimensional politics confirmed?

Although the performance of fringe parties was not as striking as in some previous local elections, there was still plenty to indicate that modern electoral competition is much more diverse and multi-dimensional than it was even 10 years ago:

- Two per cent of councils in England are now controlled by 'other parties'.
- In Scotland, the SNP won 363 seats, a net gain of 181.
- The Greens won 70 seats, a net gain of 25.
- Independent candidates were re-elected in all three mayoral contests.

Scottish Parliament elections

The third election campaign for the Scottish Parliament revolved around the following issues:

- The record of the Lib–Lab administration in Scotland, and the varying extent to which the two parties were responsible.
- The record of the Blair government at Westminster and its impact on Scotland.
- The implications of a Scot — Gordon Brown — succeeding Blair as prime minister in the months ahead.
- The constitutional implications of a victory for the Scottish National Party (SNP), which promised a referendum on whether the Scottish Parliament should have independence from Westminster. As an SNP victory was not inconceivable (though an SNP seat majority was unlikely given the use of proportional representation), the election concerned the very existence of the UK and thus excited interest well beyond Scotland's border. The results are shown in Table 2.2.

Party	Total votes	% votes	Seats won	Change from 2003
SNP	1,297,628	32.0	47	+20
Labour	1,243,789	30.6	46	−4
Conservative	618,747	15.2	17	−1
Liberal Democrat	556,903	13.7	16	−1
Green	85,555	2.1	2	−5
Others	256,404	6.3	1	−9

Turnout: 52% (+3.4% from 2003)
Further details of these results are found in Chapter 3

Table 2.2 Scottish Parliament election results, 2007

Assessing the Scottish elections: Tories irrelevant?

For David Cameron's supposedly resurgent Conservative Party, the Scottish elections were undeniably important. They were an opportunity to show it was no longer a party of southern England and was again capable of representing the whole of Britain. However, although the Tories enjoyed a few local triumphs (as in Roxburgh and Berwickshire, where their vote share rose by 11%), the results confirmed the Tories' status as a marginal party in Scotland:

- The Conservative overall vote share of 15% was again meagre, meaning that it is still not even the main opposition party in Scotland.
- Its overall vote share was slightly lower than in 2003.
- It now has one fewer Member of the Scottish Parliament (MSP) than in 2003.

For the Conservative Party to be on course for power, it needs to be the main beneficiary when the governing party flounders. This was clearly not the case at the 2007 Scottish Parliament elections.

Assessing the Scottish elections: Labour demeaned?

As the results came in, Labour officials professed to be 'pleasantly surprised'; at the start of the campaign many had predicted a 'meltdown' of Labour support. Far from being routed by the SNP, as once expected, Labour finished just one seat behind and its overall vote share fell by just 1%. Otherwise, there was scant evidence of the dominant party system thesis:

- For the first time in almost half a century, Labour lost its status as Scotland's most popular party.
- Labour lost control of the Scottish executive and entered opposition. As the SNP's Alex Salmond remarked, just before he became Scotland's new first minister: 'Labour's divine right to govern Scotland has ended.'
- Labour failed to win even a third of the votes cast.

With Labour performing so poorly in one of its traditional heartlands, its prospects of retaining support in a general election did not look strong.

Assessing the Scottish elections: Liberal Democrats diminished?

The Liberal Democrats entered the election in a position highly unusual for a third party, namely, defending its record in government as opposed to simply seeking protest votes. In view of that, the party could gain some comfort from its overall vote share rising slightly since 2003 (by 0.1%). Yet the Scottish Liberal Democrats could not be too heartened by their performance:

- Their overall vote share was still under 14%.
- They remain only the fourth most popular party in Scotland.
- Following the SNP's decision to form a minority administration, they no longer have executive power in Scotland.

It should be pointed out that the SNP did 'sound out' the Liberal Democrats with a view to forming a new 'Lib–Nat' coalition, but the Liberal Democrats rejected this on account of the SNP's separatist agenda. Yet, as commentators pointed out, if the Liberal Democrats prefer opposition to a continued share of power, this does raise doubts about whether there are three *British* parties seriously aspiring to govern.

Assessing the Scottish elections: multi-party politics confirmed?

The elections did much to strengthen the claim that, in Scotland at least, party politics is multi-dimensional, showing features of neither a two- nor three-party system:

- The SNP is now Scotland's most popular party.
- It is now Scotland's governing party, with its leader first minister.
- Its overall vote share rose by 9.6% since 2003.
- Its seat tally rose by 20.
- The Green Party won two seats.
- Twenty-seven parties fielded candidates in the elections.
- 'Other' parties and candidates (excluding the SNP, Labour, Conservative, Liberal Democrats and the Greens) polled over 256,000 votes — 6% of the total.

The use of proportional representation has certainly advanced the cause of multi-party politics in Scotland — the additional member system (AMS) being especially helpful as it allows voters to back mainstream parties in constituency contests while engaging in 'experimental voting' in the regional contests. On the other hand, the cause of Scotland's 'other parties' suffered some reverse in 2007:

- The number of Greens MSPs fell from 7 to 2.
- The Scottish Socialist Party lost all of its six seats and now has no MSPs.
- The Scottish Senior Citizens' Unity Party lost its seat and is now without any MSPs.

The Welsh Assembly elections

The Welsh Assembly campaign was similar in many ways to that of the Scottish Parliament:

- It was heavily influenced by the record of the Blair government; Labour's opponents billed the election as a 'referendum on Blairism'.
- Labour faced a threat from the nationalist party Plaid Cymru, which targeted 'core' Labour supporters — Plaid Cymru promising, among other things, a laptop for every schoolchild over the age of 11.
- Much time was spent examining the record of a Labour regime (in this case a minority Labour administration led by Rhodri Morgan).

That said, unlike in Scotland, there was no real threat to the UK — Plaid Cymru's main aim being to give the Welsh Assembly similar legislative powers to those of the Scottish Parliament. The elections were given added significance in that they were the first to be conducted since the Government of Wales Act 2006, one which strengthened the Assembly by allowing it to advance its own legislative proposals. The results are shown in Table 2.3.

Party	Total votes	% votes	Seats	Change since 2003
Labour	603,879	30.9	26	−4
Conservative	427,833	21.9	12	+1
Plaid Cymru	423,878	21.7	15	+3
Liberal Democrat	258,950	13.3	6	−
Others	238,426	12.2	1	−
Turnout: 43.5% (+5.3%)				

Table 2.3 Welsh Assembly election results, 2007

Assessing the Welsh elections: Tories reborn?

Wales is no longer the Tory-free zone it was after 1997. Thanks to proportional representation (which they once opposed), the Tories had a respectable presence in the Welsh Assembly (which they also once opposed), that has enabled them to raise their profile among Welsh voters. Following the 2007 Assembly elections, Welsh Tories were particularly pleased that they:

- remain the second most popular party in Wales, despite the vociferous campaigns of Plaid Cymru
- made some creditable gains in Clwyd West, Cardiff North and Preseli Pembrokeshire (even though this meant, under AMS, they were entitled to fewer regional seats and thus added just one to their overall seat tally)

However, it was also clear that, as in Scotland, the Tories' progress on the 'Celtic fringe' is limited, and that they are still not the sole beneficiaries of government unpopularity:

- Their vote share improved by just 2% since 2003, still representing barely a fifth of votes cast.
- They failed to take a number of 'weather vane' Labour marginals (e.g. Delyn).
- They remain only the third largest party in the Assembly.

As such, the Tories' performance in Wales did not boost their credibility as the 'alternative government' for voters across Britain.

Assessing the Welsh elections: Labour's great escape?

As in Scotland, Labour officials were upbeat after the results, claiming its support had not collapsed in the way some had predicted:

- Labour remained, by some way, the biggest party in the Assembly, with 20% more Assembly Members than its nearest rivals.
- Labour remained, by some way, the most popular party in Wales, with 9% more votes than its nearest rivals.
- Labour clung on to some marginal seats that were ferociously contested by its opponents (e.g. Caerphilly, Clwyd South).
- There was some evidence that Labour supporters, having flirted with Labour defectors, were 'coming home': Labour regained Wrexham from the

independent (and ex-Labour MP) John Marek; in Caerphilly, it saw off a
challenge from independent candidate (and ex-Labour minister) Ron Davies.
- In the short term at least, Labour remained in power after the election.

However, as in Scotland, Labour's dominance in one of its heartlands looked
fragile:
- Labour's vote share fell by over 7%, leaving it with the support of less than
a third of voters. In terms of vote share, this was Labour's worst performance
in Wales since the 1920s.
- It lost (to Plaid Cymru) the once solid Labour seat of Llanelli, which had a
majority of 16,039 at the 1997 general election.
- It failed to regain (from an independent) the once solid Labour seat of
Blaenau Gwent, which had a majority of 28,035 in 1997.
- After the election, Rhodri Morgan struggled to sustain his minority
administration. Indeed, owing to a threatened 'rainbow' coalition between
Labour's opponents, Morgan's third administration could be short-lived.

Labour's weakened grip in Wales could well portend the situation at
Westminster after the next general election.

Assessing the Welsh elections: Liberal Democrats enhanced?
As in Scotland, notions of a three-party system seemed at odds with the results
from Wales:
- The Liberal Democrats again managed to gain only 13% of votes cast.
- They were again eclipsed by another 'alternative' party — Plaid Cymru.
- They made no progress in terms of Assembly seats.

However, it is not true to say that Britain's third party is irrelevant in Wales —
especially given the near-permanence of a hung Assembly. In the wake of the
election, the Liberal Democrats were involved, first, in discussions with Rhodri
Morgan about the revival of a Lib–Lab pact, and second with Plaid Cymru and
the Tories about the possibility of a 'rainbow' coalition. On each occasion,
Liberal Democrat intransigence killed off the designs of larger parties, thus
underlining the pivotal role a third party could have in a hung parliament at
Westminster. However, as in Scotland, Liberal Democrat doubts about entering
a coalition raised questions about their seriousness as a party of government.

Assessing the Welsh elections: Plaid Cymru now poised?
Just as the SNP's performance in Scotland bolstered theories of a multi-party
system, so did the performance of Plaid Cymru in Wales:
- Plaid Cymru is again the second largest party in the Assembly.
- Its total of gained seats was the highest of any party.
- Its gain of Llanelli — once a Labour stronghold — was especially notable.
- Its vote share rose, and again exceeded a fifth of votes cast.

Plaid Cymru was duly rewarded with a taste of power. After 2 months of inter-party dealing, a coalition between Plaid Cymru and Labour emerged, with Plaid Cymru's leader, Ieuan Wyn Jones, appointed deputy first minister to Labour's Rhodri Morgan. As critics pointed out, however, this arrangement blatantly contradicted one of Plaid Cymru's key promises during the election campaign, namely, that it would not 'prop up a discredited Labour administration'.

Parliamentary by-elections

Parliamentary by-elections were held on 19 July in Ealing Southall and Sedgefield, both safe Labour seats. The one in Ealing was occasioned by the death of Labour MP Piara Khabra, while the one in Sedgefield was caused by Tony Blair's resignation from the House of Commons (immediately after he resigned as prime minister). The contest in Sedgefield was routine and uneventful. But the one in Ealing was enlivened by controversy surrounding the Tory candidate, Tony Lit, who was effectively imposed by national party officials keen to showcase a 'modern', Cameron-style Conservative. The deputy chairman of the local Tory party resigned in protest at this central interference, while Lit's position was weakened further by news that he had once donated to Labour. Table 2.4 shows the results.

Ealing Southall			
Candidate	Total votes	% votes	Change since 2005 (%)
V. Sharma (Lab)	15,188	41.0	−7.5
N. Bakhai (Lib Dem)	10,118	28.0	+4
T. Lit (Con)	8,230	22.5	+1
Others (9)	3,082	8.5	−

Labour majority: 5,070 (−6,370 since 2005)
Turnout: 43% (−13% since 2005)

Sedgefield			
Candidate	Total votes	% votes	Change since 2005 (%)
P. Wilson (Lab)	12,258	45.0	−14
G. Stone (Lib Dem)	5,572	20.0	+8
G. Robb (Con)	4,082	14.5	+0.2
Others (8)	5,780	20.5	−

Labour majority: 6,956 (−11,493 since 2005)
Turnout: 42% (−21% since 2005)

Table 2.4 Parliamentary by-elections, 2007

Assessing the by-elections: a 'Brown bounce' for Labour?

These were the first elections Labour contested under its new leader, and party officers pronounced themselves satisfied with the outcome — despite Labour's majority being halved in each case. Labour officials hinted that, given the government's unpopularity, the loss of Ealing Southall had not been inconceivable and its retention marked something of an achievement. One of Labour's post-mortem points seemed indisputable: although it was not especially popular, neither was any of its opponents.

Assessing the by-elections: 'Cameronism' in trouble?

Coming soon after Tory in-fighting over grammar schools, these results confirmed that Cameron's honeymoon as Tory leader was over. Although neither seat would normally be judged winnable for the Tories, there was a sense at the start of the campaign that, if the Tories had genuine momentum, and were again the main beneficiaries of anti-Labour feeling, Ealing was the sort of seat they could win in a by-election. Instead, they remained in third place, amid further bickering about the way their candidate was chosen (the fact that he was described on the ballot paper as 'David Cameron's Conservative' further underlined the leader's diminished allure). In Sedgefield, the Tories had absolutely no chance of winning, but were still depressed that they could not even retain the runner-up's position they held in 2005.

Assessing the by-elections: a lifeline for Campbell?

Since the May local elections, the Liberal Democrat leader had endured much speculation about his future. These results served to alleviate Campbell's position. With a 4% increased vote share in Ealing Southall, and an 8% increase in Sedgefield (where they leapfrogged the Tories into second place), the results allowed the Liberal Democrats to continue to market themselves as 'the real opposition' in many urban/Labour areas. Alas for Campbell, many Liberal Democrats still portrayed these results as being despite, rather than because of, his leadership.

The Northern Ireland Assembly elections: moderates marginalised?

When discussing UK party politics, too many students overlook Northern Ireland. Here, a very different party system has obtained throughout the post-war era.

In recent years, the province's party system has had an indisputable, multi-dimensional character. Indeed, multi-party politics was virtually institutionalised by the 1998 Good Friday Agreement, which insists on a power-sharing executive involving the two nationalist and two unionist parties. Ulster's multi-party system has also been reinforced by the use of proportional representation for Assembly elections, which has long been a feature of Northern Ireland's council and European elections, and which tends to encourage and reward smaller parties like the Greens and Alliance.

When called on to elect its revamped Assembly (a product of the 1998 Good Friday Agreement), Northern Ireland's voters underlined the province's multi-party character (see Table 2.5).

Party	Total votes*	% votes	Seats	Change from 2003
Democratic Unionist	207,721	30.1	36	+6
Sinn Féin	180,573	26.2	28	+4
Ulster Unionist	103,145	14.9	18	−9
Social Democratic and Labour	105,164	15.2	16	−2
Alliance	36,139	5.2	7	+1
Green	11,985	1.7	1	+1
Others	45,586	6.6	1#	–

*Refers to total first preference votes under the single transferable vote electoral system — see Chapter 3
#Won by an independent; in total, 17 parties fielded candidates

Table 2.5 Northern Ireland Assembly election results, 2007

Despite its multi-party character, it is clear that two of Northern Ireland's parties — the Democratic Unionist Party and Sinn Féin — are significantly stronger than the others. Ironically, the supremacy of these two parties has occurred since the Good Friday Agreement, implicitly designed to promote the two parties (Ulster Unionist Party and Social Democratic and Labour Party) with more centrist and conciliatory reputations. Not for the first time, Ulster exemplifies the law of unintended effects.

Conclusions

A number of messages emerge from the elections of 2007:

(1) Labour is unpopular. In all the elections held, Labour performed poorly; some of its vote shares were redolent of Labour's performance in 1983, when it crashed to probably its worst ever general election defeat. Labour's results strengthened the view inside the party that Tony Blair's leadership was ending at an appropriate moment, and that Labour badly needed the 'fresh start' Gordon Brown promised. Blair's allies, however, were quick to point out that Labour's electoral performance in 2007 was not notably worse than in the mid-term elections of 2003 — 2 years before it won another general election. A feature of the modern party system, perhaps, is that governing parties can expect results which, on the surface, look catastrophic, but without this having much bearing on the next general election. Voters, it seems, are more prepared than ever to deliver protest votes — and in a variety of ways.

(2) Tory progress is limited. Despite triumphs in the English council elections, Tory celebrations were tempered by the regionalised character of their progress. Indeed, the results did little to stifle complaints within the party that Cameron's 'cuddly Conservatism' failed to address the concerns of voters outside southern England. The party's limited progress in these elections led to an explosion of dissent in the summer of 2007, exemplified by the revolt against Cameron's rejection of grammar school expansion and the defection of Quentin Davies MP to Labour. In short, the 2007 elections did nothing to assist the Tory leader's efforts to rebrand his party.

(3) The Liberal Democrats have faltered. The period since 2005 has not been a glorious one for Liberal Democrats; an anti-climactic general election, an embarrassing leadership contest, and a disappointing new leader all served to deflate morale. The 2007 results pointed to no serious loss of Liberal Democrat support, but it was clear that the party had lost momentum — always a vital weapon in a third party's armoury. As a result, many Liberal Democrats were left wondering whether the dethronement of Charles Kennedy had been a serious mistake, and whether Menzies Campbell's leadership should be swiftly terminated. The outcome was a party leadership contest at the end of the year (see Chapter 9).

(4) Voters remain detached from party politics. Elections are dominated by political parties. So when voters abstain, it is usually a sign of disenchantment with party politics, and turnout in all the elections of 2007 was conspicuously low. Of particular interest was low turnout for the Scottish Parliament and Welsh Assembly elections (52% and 43% respectively). It might have been assumed that, as devolved government progressed, more Scottish and Welsh voters would be interested in the parties seeking to govern. Yet turnout in the third set of devolution elections was lower than in the first elections of 1999. Another sign of voters being turned off by parties came with the increased support for independents — candidates, in other words, who disdain any party connection (the re-election of independents in all three mayoral contests being an example).

(5) Party competition is irregular and pattern-free. The modern party battle has become increasingly localised; uniform swings of support — once a staple feature of British elections — are increasingly rare. There were innumerable examples of this in 2007, including:
- In the Scottish elections: Labour's vote share fell by 13% in Airdrie and Shotts, but rose by 22% in Falkirk West.
- In the Welsh elections: the Tories' vote share rose by 11% in Clwyd South, but fell by 15% in Ynys Mon.
- In the English council elections: Labour suffered massive losses overall but gained control of North Lincolnshire, while the Liberal Democrats lost control of Torbay but gained control of Eastbourne.

As argued in *Annual Survey 2006*, such phenomena suggest that there may no longer be a 'British party system' — just a series of variable local contests driven by local circumstances and individual reputations. Far from heralding a new epoch, party competition in the new millennium is somewhat redolent of electoral politics in the early nineteenth century.

Summary

- Despite triumphs in the English council elections, the Conservatives' performance was disappointing.
- Labour's performance was poor, but no poorer than in previous mid-term elections.
- The Liberal Democrats are 'holding their own', but have lost momentum.
- The Scottish and Welsh nationalist parties have increased in influence.
- The 2007 elections excited little interest among voters.
- Those who did vote showed no consistent patterns of party support.
- The 'true' nature of Britain's party system remains unclear.

Chapter 3

New UK electoral systems: chaos or an advance towards democracy?

About this chapter

This chapter takes the form of a debate on the experience of proportional representation (PR) in Scotland, Wales and Northern Ireland in 2007. Richard Kelly puts the case against PR. He is not impressed by the UK's new electoral systems, arguing that electoral reform has caused immense confusion, partly because it comes in various forms. For the defence, Neil Smith argues that the new PR systems used in a range of 2007 elections gave voters greater choice and delivered them the legislatures and executives that more accurately represented their choices.

The debate focuses on a key question: 'Do the UK's new electoral systems cause confusion among voters or are they an important step towards democracy?'

Richard Kelly, joint-author of this survey, is not impressed by the UK's new electoral systems

In the Rowntree Foundation's *Power* report of 2006, it was repeatedly asserted that British democracy was in 'crisis'. It was also asserted that Britain's traditional electoral system — first-past-the-post (FPTP) — was a major cause of that crisis and should be scrapped as part of any plan to improve things.

Yet, amid *Power*'s critique, it was largely forgotten that, since 1999, FPTP has not been the only electoral system used in Britain. Proportional representation (PR) has been used for elections to the European Parliament, Scottish Parliament, Welsh Assembly, London Assembly and, since this year, Scottish councils. Another type of electoral system, supplementary vote (SV), has also been used in areas with elective mayors, such as Greater London.

For those of us who defend FPTP, these elections have created a level playing field. Until the Blair era, FPTP's detractors could cite damning figures from recent British elections, while we who derided other electoral systems had to invoke evidence from abroad, thus making our arguments sound obtuse. But now, thanks to Labour's reforms, we can engage these other systems without having to play away.

Voter confusion

Our starting point is that electoral reform in the UK has caused immense confusion, partly because it comes in various forms. If you live in London, for example, you must now:

- put an x next to one party when voting in European elections
- put an x next to one party on one ballot paper, and an x next to an individual on another ballot paper, when voting in London Assembly elections
- put a first and second preference vote next to individuals when voting in mayoral elections
- still put an x next to one individual when voting for an MP

It was only a matter of time before this mélange of electoral systems caused chaos. The venue was Scotland in May 2007, when voters were asked to re-elect both their Parliament and councils, using different types of PR. 146,097 ballot papers were spoilt as a result of voters' confusion — 10 times more than when Scotland used FPTP for the 2005 general election. In many seats, the actual result was brought into question: in Edinburgh Central, for example, the winning candidate's majority was 1,193 and the number of spoilt ballot papers 1,501.

Defenders of PR later claimed it was still 'bedding in' and that voters would soon get the hang of it. But statistics suggest otherwise. In the first Scottish Parliament elections of 1999, there were just over 7,000 spoilt ballot papers in the constituency contests; by 2003 there were over 12,000; by 2007, there were over 85,000. So it seems the more PR is used, the more baffled voters become.

Counting the votes

But confusion comes not just in terms of voting; PR has also caused bewilder-ment in terms of counting. Call us old-fashioned, but FPTP supporters think it important that, in a representative democracy, voters understand how their representatives got there. Put another way, it is nice to know why one candidate was elected and another was not.

In this respect, the counting mechanisms of FPTP are pretty clear: the most popular candidate wins. Yet those of PR seem very murky — especially to voters with better things to do than study the D'Hondt formula. During the 1999 European elections, a BBC exit poll in Greater Manchester found that 'nobody' understood how votes under the new PR system were counted. During the Welsh Assembly elections of 2007, the north Wales *Daily Post* found 'hardly anyone' aware of how 'regional' seats were allocated. These are pretty damning statistics given *Power*'s claim that PR 'reconnects' voters to our political system.

Single-member constituencies

Electoral reform has also compromised one of the most admired features of British democracy: small single-member constituencies, where politicians can easily articulate the area's interests and where responsibility is clear-cut. In the European Parliament, by contrast, an English voter is now represented by up to 10 different MEPs, in diverse constituencies enfolding millions of people. In these multi-member constituencies, it is unclear which member does what. In the Scottish Parliament and Welsh Assembly, the situation is made even worse by the presence of both 'constituency' and 'regional' members, whose division of responsibility is unclear.

Party lists

PR in the UK ignores vital trends in voting behaviour, particularly the weakened link between voters and parties and the growing importance of individual candidates. In both the European and devolution elections, voters now have to endure 'closed' party lists that preclude them from backing individuals, and compel them to back one party's ranking of its candidates.

In effect, this means that the main parties' top-place candidates are guaranteed election, while those who are lower placed have no chance whatsoever (even if they fight an admirable campaign). We saw one effect of this at the last Welsh Assembly elections. The leader of the Welsh Conservatives, Nick Bourne, declined the tedious task of asking people to vote for him. Instead, he hopped to the top of a regional Tory list and thus ensured his re-election. If *Power*'s authors think that this impresses voters, they really should get out more.

Voter apathy

One of *Power*'s principal concerns was voter apathy, which it ascribed partly to FPTP's 'safe' seats. It was duly argued that new electoral systems, where 'every vote counts', would reignite voter interest. But there is little evidence that this has happened. Indeed, owing to some of the problems discussed above, electoral reform may have depressed turnout even further.

In Britain's first, nationwide PR contest — the European elections 1999 — turnout plunged to just 23%, the lowest figure ever recorded in a nationwide, British election. Although it rose at the next European elections of 2004, it was still under 40%, and not much higher than in the last European elections held under FPTP (when the EU's importance was less obvious to voters). Likewise, turnout for this year's Scottish Parliament and Welsh Assembly elections was just 52% and 43% respectively — lower than in the first devolution elections of 1999, when voters had no experience of either PR or devolved government.

Hung parliaments

The recent Welsh elections also exposed the problems of 'hung' parliaments and assemblies, which PR virtually guarantees. Had these elections been conducted under FPTP, Labour would have won a majority of seats and would have probably formed a government the next day. Instead, no party won a majority of seats, leading to over 2 months of uncertainty and inertia. The outcome highlighted an irony of PR: proportional representation in a legislature often spawns disproportional representation in an executive. The coalition eventually formed in Wales was between Labour and Plaid Cymru — yet Plaid came only third in terms of popular support, with fewer votes than the Conservatives.

But at least one good thing emerged from Britain's PR elections: they showed that if you scrap FPTP, you simply replace one imperfect system with another.

In view of these elections, it also seems that FPTP is less imperfect than its alternatives. As we conservatives say: 'If things don't change, things don't get worse.' In respect of electoral reform, it is time this principle was revived.

Neil Smith, who teaches at Manchester Grammar School with Richard Kelly, argues that voters deserve greater choice

Opponents of electoral reform rightly view the May 2007 elections in apocalyptic terms. However, this is not because the results highlighted the failings and impracticalities of proportional electoral systems, but because they saw the voters in Scotland, Wales and Northern Ireland demonstrate both their growing acceptance of PR and an increasingly sophisticated use of the different electoral systems.

Furthermore, defenders of FPTP saw another barricade fall, as the Scottish local elections used the Single Transferable Vote (STV) instead of FPTP for the first time. Only elections to Westminster and English and Welsh local elections now remain as outposts of plurality voting in the UK; factor in Gordon Brown's pledge to revitalise the British constitution, and the chances of PR being used to elect MPs at some point in the medium term look increasingly high.

Richard's rant against the effects of PR ignores the many positive outcomes of the elections, and falls back on the default position of all opponents of electoral reform: where there is partial evidence of a particular system's failings, highlight it, inflate its significance and apply this to all proportional systems. As my argument will demonstrate, any failings of the electoral systems that occurred were particular to the 2007 experience, and were significantly outweighed by the benefits to voters and parties alike.

The issue of spoilt ballots
First of all, let me deal with the 'chaos' caused by these electoral systems. The biggest problem emerged in Scotland, with a higher than expected number of spoilt ballot papers. It is important to note that the number of spoilt ballot papers was restricted to the Scottish Parliament elections only, and was an unfortunate 'one-off', due principally to the decision to include the constituency and regional votes on the same ballot paper. The Electoral Commission-instigated inquiry into the Scottish elections, headed by Ron Gould, reached the conclusion that it was chiefly the mechanics of the 2007 elections, rather than fundamental weaknesses in the operation of PR that contributed to the problems on 3 May. The evidence from the other PR elections in 2007 is that the number of invalid papers was not significantly higher than for any other election. In Wales, 0.6% of papers were spoilt, compared with 0.3% for the 2005 general election, while the use of STV for the Northern Ireland Assembly produced only 60 more invalid papers than in 2005. Although the complexity of ballot papers can lead to a higher number of spoilt ballot papers, the experience of PR in the UK is that the difference to FPTP elections is negligible.

Level of turnout

Related to this, the total level of turnout was in fact encouraging. In Scotland, turnout in the local elections was up 9.5% from the 2003 FPTP local elections. While critics are too quick to trivialise the increased turnout for the Scottish Parliament and Welsh Assembly, in both cases, the figures were in excess of the previous election, and in Wales only 'first-order' general elections have produced higher levels of voter participation since 2000. Much of the available evidence suggests that the electorate is more likely to vote when they can see the point in doing so, i.e. the institution they are electing will have a clear role and their vote will make a difference in their particular constituency. The huge increase in the number of voters using the regional list part of the ballot paper in Scotland testifies to the role of PR in satisfying this last requirement of electoral behaviour.

Increased voter choice

The increased use of STV in UK elections has contributed significantly to the extension of voter choice. In the Scottish local elections, there was a sharp increase in the average number of candidates per ward. In 2003, the average was 3.8, but in 2007 this jumped to 7.38. This extended voter choice in two ways. First, by giving the electorate a greater range of parties to choose from — the Greens, UKIP and BNP all contested a greater number of wards than in 2003. Second, it provided voters with a choice *within* parties, empowering the voter to influence which party candidate was elected, instead of having the party choice imposed on them, as happens under FPTP.

Voter choice was also extended by the complete absence of uncontested wards in the Scottish local elections. This was in sharp contrast to England, where the single member wards that are characteristic of FPTP frequently deprive voters of the right to choose between competing candidates. Simply examining the statistics for one district council, Lichfield, demonstrates the (less than) wonderful democratic credentials of FPTP: voters in 9 of the 56 council wards were faced with an uncontested election.

Multi-member constituencies

Critics of PR are quick to point out that multi-member constituencies destroy the sacred link between MP and constituent. However, skilful voter management by the parties, principally through the operation of *bailiwicking* agreements in Scotland helped prevent this occurring. Where parties fielded more than one candidate per ward in the Scottish local elections, candidates tended to enter into agreements dividing up the ward. While the initial impetus to this behaviour was certainly the avoidance of intra-party competition, it also contributed to the preservation of one of the stronger features of FPTP. Of course, supporters of the additional member system (AMS) would also point to the continuing existence of constituency MPs under that system, and the existence of a 'bonus' MP provided courtesy of the list vote.

Fairness

The 2007 elections scored highly on fairness criteria. While it is true that PR elections tend to result in coalitions, and some take several weeks to assemble, is that really less desirable than subjecting the electorate to the tyranny of a minority? In 2005, Labour polled barely 35% of the vote, yet enjoy a 66-seat majority in the House of Commons. If FPTP had been used to elect all members of the Welsh Assembly, it would have won 60% of the seats on 32% of the vote. This situation would have been repeated in Scotland where Labour, who polled *less* than the SNP on both constituency and regional votes, would have been able to form a majority administration if the election had been held using FPTP alone. As it is, the SNP has formed a minority executive, which is not only consistent with the wishes of the electorate, but also enhances the power of the Scottish Parliament. Unlike Westminster, Scotland has bidden farewell to the notion of an 'elective dictatorship'.

I wonder if the leader of the Conservative Party might also look positively at the results of the 2007 elections? In August 2006, David Cameron announced that there was a need for 'proper representation of women and black and ethnic minority candidates in Parliament', and immediately came under fire for his decision to impose 50% female shortlists on Conservative constituency associations. The experiences of PR in 2007 suggest that he might be more able to achieve greater diversity of MPs through electoral reform. In Northern Ireland, STV brought the election of the first black and minority ethnic MLA, and increased the number of female members to 19. This pattern could also be seen in Scotland, where the list vote produced the first black and minority ethnic MSP, and 33% female MSPs, and in Wales, where 47% of Assembly members are women. Westminster, by the way, has 128 female MPs — 19% of the total.

So, several good things came out of the UK's elections in 2007. Voters were given greater choice in who they could vote for, their choices were more accurately represented in the composition of the legislatures and executives, and their representatives more closely reflect the diverse cultures in which voters live. As we democrats say: 'Of the people, by the people, for the people.'

Summary

Much seems to depend on what an electoral system is *for*, a question for which there is no definitive answer. If an electoral system's prime role is thought to be 'strong', ready-made government, then events after the Welsh and Scottish elections will have underlined the case for FPTP. However, if an electoral system is meant to produce a 'representative' outcome, reflecting voting patterns, then the 2007 elections may represent a clear vindication of electoral reform.

Chapter 4

The battle for the Labour leadership: a pointless contest?

About this chapter

It was once said that a change of Tory leader was 'swift and surprising'.
This could certainly not be said about the change of Labour's leadership in 2007.
The transfer of power from Blair to Brown was prolonged and tortuous, even
though the outcome was seldom in doubt. This chapter charts the end of Blair's
leadership of the party and the eventual 'coronation' of Gordon Brown. It also
recalls the contest for the deputy leadership — one which revealed serious
problems with the way Labour selects its leaders. The chapter addresses key
questions, such as:

- What impact did Blair's announcement that he would not seek a fourth term
  have on his leadership?
- Why did the Labour Party decide to have a coronation rather than a contest?
- Did the deputy leadership campaign represent a lurch to the left?
- What are the merits and problems of Labour's electoral college system?
- Has the status of Labour's deputy leader been undermined?

Blair: staying or going?

When Tony Blair resigned as both Labour leader and prime minister on
27 June 2007, it was one of the least surprising resignations in recent political
history. Indeed, it had been pending since October 2004, when Blair
announced (ahead of the last general election) that he would not seek a fourth
term as prime minister — an announcement that, he believed, would help
unite the party and secure a third Labour victory.

However, during both the 2005 election campaign and its aftermath, there was
inevitable speculation about how much of a third term Blair would serve.
Largely because of the Iraq debacle (and polls showing that Labour won
despite, not because of, Blair), increasing numbers of Labour MPs felt Blair
should not serve a full third term and should resign as quickly as possible. It
was argued that the party was in urgent need of a fresh start, and that Blair's
successor needed ample time to 'bed in' before the general election of 2009/10.

For about a year after the 2005 general election, Blair remained mischievously
evasive about his departure date. However, events in the autumn of 2006
conspired to force his hand. For example:
- Seventeen Labour MPs wrote to Blair asking him to resign 'within a year'.

- Tom Watson (one of the letter's signatories) resigned as junior defence minister, claiming that Blair's leadership was now 'hindering' the government.
- Seven parliamentary private secretaries (Khalid Mahmood, Wayne David, Ian Lucas, Mark Tami, Chris Mole, David Wright and Iain Wright) resigned for similar reasons.

In response to such pressures, Blair announced that the 2006 Labour conference would be the last he attended as leader. Yet two key questions remained unanswered as 2007 dawned:

- When exactly would Blair resign? For example, before or after the May elections?
- Would Brown have a rival for the leadership?

For the first few months of 2007, these questions seemed to preoccupy and cripple the Labour Party, precluding any systematic response to the resurgent Conservative Party. Indeed, during the early months of 2007, the contest between the parties seemed less pressing than the debates going on within the Labour Party.

January–June: who is leading Labour?

On 16 January 2007, Blair declared he was 'far from finished yet', and stated his intention to complete a number of public service reforms, lead Labour into the May elections, revive the Good Friday Agreement in Ulster and attend a June summit of EU leaders. It was even rumoured Blair might delay his resignation until the autumn, making the 2007 Labour conference a culmination of the ensuing leadership contest.

Eventually, Blair announced his resignation on 10 May to his Constituency Labour Party in Sedgefield, and pledged his support for Gordon Brown. On the same day, John Prescott announced his own resignation as deputy leader, confirming that the leadership contest would be a two-pronged affair.

During the early part of 2007, Brown tried to raise his profile as prime minister-in-waiting by identifying himself with a wider range of political issues. He promised a 'new style of government', a 'new respect for Parliament', an 'end to spin' and an emphasis on 'Britishness' (along with a quest to define it). In foreign affairs, too, Brown struck a more statesmanlike posture — touring India, backing its bid for membership of the UN Security Council and invoking a 'new world order', giving greater priority to the elimination of poverty.

All this, of course, created some confusion as to where power really lay. Was Blair now prime minister in name only? Did the distinction between Blair and Brown now represent a modern version of what Bagehot termed the 'dignified' and 'efficient' sides of our constitution (the former representing the formal, ceremonial side of government; the latter reality and power)?

Throughout this Labour government, there have been claims that we had 'dyarchical' government, headed not by one but two politicians. The last months of Blair's premiership dramatically underlined this phenomenon.

Contest or coronation?

Within the Labour Party, there were always split views on whether Brown should face a challenge for the leadership. Those who favoured a contest included Brown himself, who argued that:

- It would make his accession look more democratic and legitimate.
- It would allow a much-needed debate about the party's future direction.
- It would permit the chancellor to outline his vision of politics beyond economics.

However, other Brown supporters, such as Diane Abbott MP, feared a contest would expose divisions inside the party and advertise the extent of opposition to the new leader.

In January, left-wing MPs John McDonnell and Michael Meacher declared a wish to stand, both believing they could obtain the necessary number of nominations (45) from fellow MPs. Both made it clear they had no genuine ambitions to lead the party. They had no fundamental objections to Brown taking over; they simply believed the party would benefit from the formality of a debate and a ballot.

Stop Gordon?

Yet there were other elements in the party that favoured a contest for a more profound reason: the belief that Brown might not be 'up to' the job of prime minister. This view was fuelled by assorted Blairites who whispered about the chancellor's 'psychological flaws', his 'control freakery', his belief that 'disagreement equals disloyalty' and his 'autocratic' way of doing business at the Treasury. In addition, there were fears that, if the government really needed a makeover, then Brown — co-architect of New Labour and chancellor for the last 10 years — was not the obvious candidate.

As a result, there were rumours of a more serious challenge, with three names widely touted:

- John Reid, the home secretary
- Charles Clarke, the former home secretary
- David Miliband, trade and industry secretary

Of these three candidates, Miliband excited by far the most interest. Young and personable, he was widely seen as the 'heir to Blair', able (like Blair 10 years earlier) to reach beyond Labour's natural constituency. He was helped further by the fact he was not widely known to voters — a considerable asset if the government wished to reinvent itself after 10 years in power. Several opinion polls suggested that Labour under Miliband would fare better than under

Brown, while Tories acknowledged that a Miliband premiership posed diffi-culties. The freshnesss of their own new leader would have been countered and, as a Cameron insider admitted, 'we've only prepared for Gordon…there's no Plan B' (*Daily Telegraph*, 4 April 2007).

Coronation confirmed

By the start of May, however, it was clear that Brown would, after all, have an unopposed succession. After weeks of speculation, Miliband confirmed that he would not be a contender, instead offering his support for Brown. On 3 May, Clarke and Reid did likewise. The only remaining question was whether there would be a token contest, which depended on whether McDonnell or Meacher could summon enough backing from Labour MPs. By 14 May, Meacher declared he could not get the support needed and that he would now assist McDonnell's quest for nomination.

By the time nominations closed on 17 May, it was clear that McDonnell's quest had failed too (he secured only 29 nominations). Brown, meanwhile, secured 308 nominations from MPs (87%) and endorsement from 407 of the Constituency Labour Parties (65%). So the scale of Brown's affirmation was huge — even though it had threatened not to be just 2 months earlier.

The deputy leadership campaign: a lurch to the left?

With the leadership resolved, attention focused on the race to become Brown's deputy. As expected, this attracted wider interest, with six candidates eventually securing the 45 nominations required (see Table 4.1).

Candidate	Number of MP nominations
Alan Johnson	73
Harriet Harman	65
Peter Hain	51
Jon Cruddas	49
Hazel Blears	49
Hilary Benn	47

Table 4.1 Nominations for the deputy leadership

Among those not included were left-winger Jeremy Corbyn (who had expressed an interest in December 2006), Ed Balls, Patricia Hewitt and Jack Straw (all of whom were mentioned as possible candidates in newspapers, without explicitly declaring an interest).

During the 7-week campaign for the deputy leadership, it seemed as if the contest was split between three candidates wishing to take the party back to a left-wing comfort zone (Harman, Cruddas, Hain), and three candidates offering a robust defence of New Labour (Blears, Johnson, Benn). As such, the campaign featured a number of leftist themes redolent of Labour in the pre-Blair era. For example:

- scepticism about private-sector engagement in public services
- enthusiasm for reducing inequality, redistributing wealth and increasing progressive taxation
- demands for the re-empowerment of trade unions

All this suggested that, despite 13 years of Blairism, the Labour Party was not wholly reconstructed and that the ethos of New Labour might not survive its main creator.

A summary of the candidates' policies is set out in Table 4.2.

Candidate	Position held at time of contest	Policies
Hilary Benn	International development secretary	Blair loyalist, emphasised the need to tackle global poverty, wanted an end to charitable status for private schools, defensive about the government's record in Iraq
Alan Johnson	Education secretary	Blair loyalist, favoured a clear continuation with the themes of New Labour, keen on more private involvement in public services, robust defender of the Iraq War and cautious about withdrawal, keen to stress the importance of 'alternative' family structures (in contrast to Tory support for a marriage tax allowance)
Hazel Blears	Labour Party chair	Blair ultra-loyalist, defended 'aspirational values' and warned against tax increases, unequivocally supportive of government policy since 1997
Harriet Harman	Constitutional affairs minister	Advocated 'wealth tax' and Royal Commission on wealth redistribution, regretted the Iraq War (having once supported it), opposed faith schools, stressed the case for more gender equality and family-friendly policies in the workplace
Peter Hain	Northern Ireland and Wales secretary	Argued the case for 'democratising' Labour's policy-making process and more grass-roots influence in government decisions, called for a review of Tory trade union reforms, critical of privatisation in health and education
Jon Cruddas	MP	Self-styled champion of Labour backbenchers and Constituency Labour Party members, keen on party reorganisation and increased grass-roots influence, effusive about 'core Labour values', opposed to private sector involvement in the NHS, opposed the renewal of Trident

Table 4.2 The deputy leadership campaign: candidates' policies

What were the merits of Labour's selection system?

For the sixth time since its formation in 1981, Labour's deputy leadership contest involved an electoral college system (see Box 4.1). Under this system, a third of the votes are granted to MPs/MEPs, a third to Constituency Labour Party (CLP) members, and a third to members of affiliated organisations (chiefly trade unions).

> **Box 4.1** **Choosing a deputy leader 2007: the mechanics**
>
> **1** Candidates seek nomination from 12.5% of Labour MPs
>
> **2** The electoral college:
>
> **354 MPs and 19 MEPs = third of votes**
> *(each individual's vote = approx 0.089% of electoral college)*
>
> **Approx 200,000 CLP members = third of votes**
> *(each individual's vote = approx 0.00017% of electoral college)*
>
> **Approx 3 million affiliated members* = third of votes**
> *(each individual's vote = approx 0.00001% of electoral college)*
>
> *The affiliated members are drawn from 48 societies and trade unions.

In some ways, the deputy leadership contest of 2007 was a triumph for party democracy:

- Almost 3.5 million ballot papers were distributed by Labour headquarters and the affiliated organisations. In terms of voters, it was one of the most democratic leadership contests ever held in this country.
- With a dozen or so hustings across the country, there were ample opportunities for ordinary members to listen and question the candidates.
- Unlike in some previous Labour leadership contests (1981, 1988, 1992), there was no block voting; the principle of one person, one vote was upheld.
- Votes within each section of the college would be aggregated nationally — rather than on a union-by-union, or CLP-by-CLP basis. This ensured that minority views within a union or CLP were not eclipsed.
- The system allowed voters a wide choice of candidates — unlike the Conservative Party's system, which gives constituency members only an either/or choice (see *Annual Survey 2006*, pp. 58–63).
- The use of the alternative vote electoral system ensured the winning candidate would have majority support (see Table 4.3).

What were the problems of Labour's selection system?

- The principle of one person, one vote did not always apply: for example, a CLP member who was also a trade unionist had two votes, while MPs like Gillian Merron — a member of both a CLP and the UNISON trade union — had three.
- Owing to the differing size of the college's sections, not all votes were of equal weight — the vote of an individual MP being infinitely more influential than that of a constituency member (see Box 4.1).

- Enfranchising CLPs was a costly exercise for Labour headquarters, at a time when it was facing debts of over £20 million. A number of activists stated they 'would sooner the party sort out its finances, and make sure we can fight the next election properly…instead of spending thousands on determining a deputy leader who probably won't be that important' (*Guardian*, 8 June).
- As a result of the numbers involved, the contest was lengthy — 7 weeks — and some felt it distracted Labour from the business of government. In the days when a contest involved only a few hundred MPs, it could be completed much more expeditiously.
- The affiliated section led to various anomalies:
  - Most affiliated members did not have the interests of the Labour Party at heart, and many would have voted for other parties in the 2005 general election (an example being Roger Gale, member of the broadcasting union BECTU and a Conservative MP for Thanet North). It seemed perverse that such affiliated members had, cumulatively, as much weight as those who were actively involved in the party's affairs.
  - Most affiliated members had no interest in participating — and only 8% did (see Table 4.3).
  - Affiliated organisations spent considerable sums balloting a largely indifferent membership. In the union's newsletters, members of USDAW (the shopworkers' union) seemed uniformly angry that £70,000 of USDAW funds were 'squandered' in this way.

The results

The outcome of the deputy leadership contest was announced at a special conference on 24 June, 3 days before Gordon Brown formally became prime minister.

	MPs/MEPs	CLPs	Affiliated members	Total
1st round				
Harman	6.54	8.04	4.35	18.9
Johnson	8.08	5.53	4.55	18.2
Cruddas	4.63	5.67	9.09	19.4
Benn	4.27	7.21	4.93	16.4
Hain	4.81	3.87	6.64	15.3
Blears	4.99	3.01	3.77	11.8 (*eliminated*)*
2nd round				
Harman	7.29	8.80	5.15	21.2
Johnson	11.47	6.35	5.91	23.7
Cruddas	4.74	6.01	9.64	20.4
Benn	4.74	7.93	5.56	18.2
Hain	5.1	4.24	7.08	16.4 (*eliminated*)

	MPs/MEPs	CLPs	Affiliated members	Total
3rd round				
Harman	8.61	10.15	7.12	25.9
Johnson	12.78	7.31	7.81	27.9
Cruddas	6.30	6.58	11.01	23.9
Benn	5.65	9.29	7.39	22.3 (*eliminated*)
4th round				
Harman	10.29	13.82	9.46	33.6
Johnson	15.39	10.71	10.25	36.4
Cruddas	7.65	8.81	13.61	30.1 (*eliminated*)
Final round				
Harman	15.42	18.83	16.18	50.43 (*elected*)
Johnson	17.91	14.50	17.15	49.56
Total votes cast/turnout	**367 (99%)**	**96,756 (54%)**	**215,604 (8%)**	**312,727 (54%)**

*Under the rules of the alternative vote electoral system, when a candidate was eliminated, the secondary preferences of his/her supporters were transferred to the remaining candidates.

Table 4.3 Results of Labour's deputy leadership contest, 2007 (%)

Conclusion: what were the implications of the results?

(1) Gordon Brown's position was unassailable. As the first Labour leader to secure the position unopposed, Brown was in a uniquely strong position to impose his will on the party. Helped by the ministerial departure of 'big beasts' like John Reid, Brown seemed to have complete domination of his government. Unlike the cabinets of Blair, Major and Thatcher, Brown's contained no serious rival to his leadership in the short term. The only long-term brake on Brown seemed to be David Miliband, whose raised profile Brown acknowledged by making him one of the youngest-ever foreign secretaries.

(2) Harriet Harman's mandate was limited. This can be shown in three ways:
- She was not, initially, the most popular candidate. If the election had been held under the first-past-the-post system, Jon Cruddas would now be deputy leader of the Labour Party.
- In all five ballots, she was not the first choice of Labour MPs — a serious failing, given that MPs usually have a better knowledge of the candidates than any other section of the party.
- Among affiliated members, too, Harman never topped the poll: in the first ballot she came second from bottom.

In short, Harman owed her victory to just one section of the electoral college: CLP members. Small wonder that Brown felt able to deny her the position of deputy prime minister (which her predecessor enjoyed), leaving the status of

deputy leader much weaker than it had been under Blair. Indeed, this made some question the point of the whole contest. As *The Times* commented (26 June), 'The best that can be said of the contest is that it is over.'

Summary

- Brown's accession was not seamless, but eventually emphatic.
- The contest raised the profile of David Miliband as leader-in-waiting.
- The problems of Labour's electoral college were again exposed.
- Harman's victory in the deputy leader contest was a hollow one.
- The status of Labour's deputy leader has been undermined.

Chapter 5

The EU Reform Treaty: should there be a referendum?

About this chapter

In June 2007, a summit held under the German presidency of the European Union resulted in the drafting of a new EU Reform Treaty. This agreement represented the first concerted effort to break the stalemate that had gone on for 2 years, following the rejection of the 400-page draft EU constitution by voters in referendums held in France and Holland in June 2005.

UK voters had been promised their own referendum on the original constitution. This chapter focuses on the arguments surrounding whether UK ratification of the EU Reform Treaty that replaced this constitution should similarly be made dependent on the outcome of a nationwide referendum. In particular, this chapter addresses questions such as:

- Why was this new treaty drafted in the summer of 2007?
- How significant are the differences between the original draft constitution and this new treaty?
- Are calls for a referendum motivated more by political opportunism than by the terms of the treaty?
- What precedents exist regarding the use of referendums in such circumstances?

Why was the EU Reform Treaty drafted in the summer of 2007?

The enlargement of the EU from 15 to 27 member states between 2004 and 2007 necessitated a major reworking of EU institutions and procedures. This reorganisation was left in a state of flux, however, when the majority of voters in referendums held in France and Holland in June 2005 opted to oppose ratifying the draft EU constitution.

Prominent voices on either side of the enlargement debate initially welcomed the 'pause for reflection' afforded by these poll reversals. By the summer of 2006, however, critics were claiming that this year-long interval had in fact been 'all pause and no reflection', as Anthony Browne of the *The Times* put it.

The stalemate was in part a product of the unpalatability of the various options available to Europe's leading players (see Box 5.1). Maintaining the status quo (option 3) was simply not feasible in an enlarged union of 27 states. Neither was there any real appetite for options 1 or 2, with public opinion in countries such as France and the UK still said to be set against a formal constitution.

> ### Box 5.1 The EU constitution: what are the options?
>
> **1** Revive the constitution and submit it to fresh referendums in those countries where it was rejected.
>
> **2** Redraft the constitution so as to address the concerns that had provoked opposition.
>
> **3** Abandon plans for a new constitution and persist with existing arrangements.
>
> **4** Proceed with those aspects of the new constitution that do not require formal ratification, and leave the more thorny questions until a later date.

By the spring of 2007, therefore, it had become apparent that option 4 offered the only realistic way forward. In an approach dubbed 'Nice plus' by some observers — a reference to the 2001 Treaty of Nice — progress would have to be made through ad hoc agreements or by amending existing treaties; an altogether more modest rejigging of the EU than that originally envisaged by the constitution. Thus, in March 2007, the German chancellor Angela Merkel expressed her hope that a 'charter', some 80% smaller than the 2004 constitution, could be in place by February 2008.

By April 2007, however, the debate had moved on significantly with Tony Blair's suggestion that much of what had originally been set out in the constitution could be achieved by the means of an 'amending treaty', thereby removing the need for ratification by referendum in the various member states. It was this concept of an amending treaty that ultimately became a reality in the form of the EU Reform Treaty agreed in Germany in June 2007.

Was the EU Reform Treaty of 2007 really that different from the draft constitution rejected by the French and the Dutch in 2005?

Although references to the EU flag and anthem that were present in the 2004 constitution were dropped in the 2007 Reform Treaty, other key elements of the constitution survived largely in their original form (see Table 5.1).

Although the then prime minister Tony Blair secured a UK opt-out in the sphere of justice and home affairs, as well as a separate legally binding protocol preventing the Charter of Fundamental Rights from having full legal force in the UK, it was clear that the Reform Treaty would, in virtually all other respects, be indistinguishable from the constitution it replaced. Indeed, according to the *Guardian* on 22 August, Valéry Giscard d'Estaing, one of the key architects of the original constitution, saw the changes between the two documents as 'few and far between…and more cosmetic than real'. The

Area	EU constitution 2004	EU Reform Treaty 2007
Form	Over 400 pages. Sought to bring together existing treaties into a single authoritative (codified) document that would set out the rules of the EU.	277 pages. Achieved necessary changes by amending the Treaty of Rome and the Treaty on the European Union (Maastricht), as opposed to creating a new codified 'rulebook' for the EU.
The EU presidency	An EU president elected by the European Council for a single, renewable term of $2\frac{1}{2}$ years. Subject to approval by the EU Parliament.	Provision retained.
Council of Ministers' use of qualified majority voting (QMV)	The use of QMV to be extended into a number of areas previously requiring unanimity. A qualified vote to be defined as one where at least 55% of the members of the Council (at least 15) and representing member states comprising at least 65% of the EU population approve. Known as the 'double-majority' system.	Provision retained, with this new 'double majority' system to be phased in between 2014 and 2017.
The Commission	To consist of one national from each member state for an initial term of 5 years. Thereafter, a number equal to half of the number of member states.	Retained, with the '$\frac{1}{2}$ formula' to be introduced from 2014.
The European Parliament	Extension of co-decision procedure, under which decision-making power is shared between the EU Parliament and the Council of Ministers.	Provision retained.
Charter of Fundamental Rights	Codifies the existing rights and freedoms enjoyed by citizens of the EU.	Provision retained, without extending the powers of the EU.
Foreign and defence policy	Greater cooperation on foreign affairs and defence. The appointment of an EU minister of foreign affairs to conduct the EU Common Foreign and Security Policy.	Provision retained, in essence, but with a 'High Representative of the Union for Foreign Affairs and Security Policy' as opposed to a 'Union Minister of Foreign Affairs'.

Table 5.1 Retained or reworked? The constitution and the Reform Treaty compared

decision to create a post of 'High Representative of the Union for Foreign Affairs and Security Policy' as opposed to that of 'Minister of Foreign Affairs', envisaged in the original constitution, was certainly viewed widely as a change in presentation as opposed to substance.

Are calls for a referendum motivated more by political opportunism than by the substance of the treaty?

Calls for UK ratification of the treaty to be subject to a nationwide referendum resulted largely from the obvious similarities between the new document and the constitution that it replaced. Put simply, if the Reform Treaty was just 'the constitution by another name', should UK ratification not be made dependent on the outcome of the kind of public poll as promised in the case of the original document? Universal acceptance of this view would certainly have made opposition to a referendum hard to justify. In public at least, however, some were prepared to argue that the two documents were sufficiently different to remove the need for such a referendum.

For the Liberal Democrats, Sir Menzies Campbell appeared to agree with the government's view that a referendum was not required, arguing on 14 September that it was a 'comparatively minor treaty'. Though some saw this as an attempt to avoid a likely referendum defeat over a measure favoured by his own party, such a view was undermined by Campbell's suggestion that there should instead be a public referendum on the far more central issue of the UK's continued membership of the EU. 'It [was] time,' he argued, 'to end the shadow boxing...and to have an honest debate on the future of Europe.'

Conservative support for a referendum was ostensibly based on their contention that the Reform Treaty was the constitution in all but name. However, their support for a public vote also had the benefit of creating greater unity within their own ranks, while at the same time putting Gordon Brown on the back foot during a period when the new premier and his party were enjoying a healthy lead in the polls. Some questioned whether the Conservatives' resistance to further political integration within the EU was not at odds with their opposition to economic protectionism — how could the party be so fearful of supposed European interference in UK affairs, while at the same time remain happy to see UK companies taken over by foreign interests?

The Conservatives were joined in their support for a referendum by an unlikely ally — the Trades Union Congress (TUC). The TUC's primary concern was the UK opt-out from the Charter of Fundamental Rights, which would see citizens in the other 26 member states being granted enhanced rights in respect of industrial action. However, many delegates at the TUC conference in September 2007 were also keen to see the government honouring its 2005 commitment to hold a referendum on the original constitution. The possibility of some kind of pro-referendum 'marriage of convenience' between the TUC and the Conservatives appeared more likely when senior Tory John Redwood, much to the horror of those on the left of the TUC, made a public offer of cooperation.

Far more worrying for Gordon Brown would have been the extent to which public opinion and the opinions of those on the Labour backbenches appeared by the autumn of 2007 to be moving in favour of a public vote. A poll in the *Daily Telegraph* on 20 August showed that 80% of the general public favoured a popular vote. More significant, perhaps, was the fact that in the same poll, one in four Labour voters said that they would not vote for a Brown government if he denied them such a referendum.

In a similar vein, *The Economist* (1 September) quoted Ian Davidson as saying that as many as 120 of his fellow Labour MPs — and not all of them backbenchers — favoured a referendum. Justice secretary Jack Straw was said to be one of those who privately favoured a public vote.

In the light of this opposition within his own party and the unlikelihood of his securing further concessions over the Reform Treaty (see Box 5.2), the Liberal Democrats' decision to come out against a referendum was certainly fortuitous.

Box 5.2 **Prospects for further concessions**

Labour backbencher Ian Davidson says that he won't push for a referendum if Mr Brown secures 12 big changes to the treaty, including scrapping the EU's foreign policy representative.

However, Mr Brown's chances of winning any more concessions look very slim. Many in Brussels and among the more integrationist member states believe Britain secured an irritatingly favourable deal in June. And whereas Mr Blair was generally regarded as a good European, Mr Brown enjoys little favour in the EU.

Source: adapted from 'Brown's referendum dilemma — to vote or not to vote', *The Economist*, 1 September 2007.

What precedents exist regarding the use of referendums in such circumstances?

It has been over 60 years since the then prime minister Clement Attlee described referendums as devices 'alien to our traditions'. Since then, of course, Parliament has approved a number of referendums, and the three main UK parties have become accustomed to offering manifesto commitments to such popular votes on a range of issues.

While Tony Blair claimed that Tory calls for a public vote over the Reform Treaty were 'utterly absurd', such a referendum would hardly be unprecedented. The UK has already held one referendum on the question of Europe (then the EEC, in 1975) and the nation has previously been promised votes ahead of the proposed UK adoption of the euro and, more recently, the ratification of the EU constitution. Indeed, whereas other nations regularly hold referendums on issues ranging from the availability of abortion to their membership of NATO, all nine referendums sanctioned by the UK Parliament since 1973 (see Table 5.2) have concerned relations between the various tiers of government affecting UK citizens: subnational, national, and supranational.

When?	Where?	What?
1973	Northern Ireland	Should Northern Ireland stay in the UK?
1975	UK	Should the UK stay in the EEC?
1979	Scotland	Should there be a Scottish Parliament?
1979	Wales	Should there be a Welsh Parliament?
1997	Scotland	Should there be a Scottish Parliament? With tax varying powers?
1997	Wales	Should there be a Welsh Assembly?
1998	London	Should there be a London mayor and London Assembly?
1998	Northern Ireland	Approval for the Good Friday Agreement.
2004	The northeast	Should there be a regional assembly for the northeast?

Table 5.2 UK referendums since 1973

Although the lack of a codified constitution means that we have no formal list of circumstances in which referendums are legally required, it has long been accepted that such votes can and probably should be called in respect of major constitutional changes. This convention, allied to the fact that a referendum was promised in the case of the earlier EU constitution, means that the question of whether there should be a referendum over the Reform Treaty is totally dependent on one's assessment of the scope and scale of changes it brings to the EU, i.e. just how different it is from the original constitution (see Table 5.1).

Conclusions

Many politicians and citizens across the EU were clearly concerned that the original draft constitution would have represented a step too far along the road to a 'United States of Europe'. It is not surprising, therefore, that these concerns were simply transferred to the treaty negotiated following the failure of efforts to ratify this constitution; particularly in light of the fact that the second document bore such a striking resemblance to the first.

Against this backdrop, the EU-wide clamour for ratifying referendums in relation to the 2007 Reform Treaty is hardly surprising. What is more puzzling, however, is the failure of the treaty's critics to come up with a tenable alternative vision of how an enlarged EU might be made to work in the absence of the necessary structural and procedural changes to the EU that were common to both documents. This, surely, is the key question for a union in which even the most practical of problems, for example translation (see Box 5.3), has the capacity to bring things to a standstill.

Box 5.3 Lost in translation

Costs [related to interpreters] have soared since the 'big bang' enlargement of 2004, when the number of member states grew from 15 to 25 and the number of working languages almost doubled from 11 to 20. Intepretation for a full-day meeting in the parliament, which cost £25,000 before enlargement, now costs £59,000.

The interpretation service is dwarfed by the translation service, which employs 2,000 people [translating] EU documents into every working language. This has to be done by law, although the full service has been suspended for the last 2 years because the EU has not been able to hire enough Maltese translators after the tiny Mediterranean island joined in 2004.

Source: adapted from Nicholas Watt, 'Lost in translation: £17 million of taxpayers' money for EU interpreters who are not needed', *Guardian*, 31 August 2006.

Summary

- The EU Reform Treaty of 2007 sought to bring about many of the changes originally proposed in the draft EU constitution of 2004.
- EU leaders hoped that their decision to negotiate an amending treaty, as opposed to a new constitution, might remove the need for the kind of national referendums that had resulted in the failure to ratify the original constitution in 2005.
- Despite such hopes, the UK government came under intense pressure to hold a referendum in 2007 — as all three major parties had promised to do before ratifying the original constitution.
- Although some of those calling for a referendum were clearly attracted to the cause by the prospect of embarrassing the government, others were motivated by the obvious similarities between the original constitution and the new treaty.

Chapter 6

A Supreme Court for the UK: what difference will it make?

About this chapter

At the start of the legal year in October 2009, the 12 Law Lords who comprise the House of Lords Appellate Committee — the highest UK court of appeal — will move to new accommodation in the renovated Middlesex Guildhall, opposite the Houses of Parliament. Though they will remain members of the House of Lords, they will at the same time become the first Justices of the new UK Supreme Court.

The creation of a UK Supreme Court was one of many measures set out in the Constitutional Reform Act 2005 and discussed in *Annual Survey 2006*. This chapter examines precisely what the Supreme Court will be like and what it will mean for the UK. In particular, the following questions are considered:

- What jurisdiction and powers will the Supreme Court have?
- How will appointments to the Court be made?
- Will the creation of the Court enhance the independence of the judiciary?
- Will the Supreme Court be similar to its US counterpart?

What jurisdiction and powers will the Supreme Court have?

The 12 Lords of Appeal in Ordinary (the Law Lords) who sit on the Appellate Committee of the House of Lords have traditionally performed a role similar to US Supreme Court Justices — hearing appeals and thereby clarifying the meaning of contentious points of law. Consequently, British politics textbooks often refer to the House of Lords as the UK's 'Supreme Court', though such a label can lead to confusion; not least among those failing to grasp fully the difference between the *legislative* work of the upper chamber and the *judicial* work of the Appellate Committee.

The fact that the UK's highest court of appeal is hidden away within the legislature has further denied UK citizens the kind of iconic and independent Supreme Court enjoyed by those in the USA (see Box 6.1). The creation of a UK Supreme Court, benefiting from an independent appointments process and accommodated in a separate building, will go some way towards addressing such criticisms. At the same time, the confusion that might result from the fact that the Court of Appeal, the High Court and the Crown Court are also known formally as the 'Supreme Court of England and Wales' will be resolved by renaming them the 'Senior Courts of England and Wales', with the

'Supreme Court of Judicature of Northern Ireland' becoming the 'Court of Judicature of Northern Ireland'.

Box 6.1 **In search of the UK Supreme Court**

Ask any tour guide in Washington DC and they will be able to direct you to the US Supreme Court. Make the same enquiry of a London guide about the UK version and they would be left scratching their head.

Source: Chris Summers, 'Grand Designs' BBC News (online), 7 March 2007.

Under the Constitutional Reform Act 2005 (CRA), the UK Supreme Court will take on the four roles previously performed by the Law Lords. These are:

- To act as the final court of appeal in England, Wales and Northern Ireland.
- To hear appeals on issues of public importance surrounding arguable points of law.
- To hear appeals from civil cases in England, Wales, Northern Ireland and Scotland.
- To hear appeals from criminal cases in England, Wales and Northern Ireland (the High Court of Justiciary will retain jurisdiction over criminal cases in Scotland).

In addition, the Court will take on the role that the Judicial Committee of the Privy Council has performed in resolving disputes between the UK Parliament and the devolved governments of Northern Ireland, Scotland and Wales. However, the Privy Council Committee will still retain jurisdiction over Commonwealth cases.

How will appointments to the Supreme Court be made?

The first Justices of the new Supreme Court will be the 12 Law Lords in post at the time of the move into the new accommodation in October 2009 (see Box 6.2). The most senior of the 12 will take on the role of President of the Court, with the second most senior assuming the role of Deputy President.

Box 6.2 **The 12 Law Lords in post in December 2007 (in order of seniority)**

1 Lord Bingham of Cornhill	7 Lord Walker of Gestingthorpe
2 Lord Hoffmann	8 Baroness Hale of Richmond
3 Lord Hope of Craighead	9 Lord Carswell
4 Lord Saville of Newdigate	10 Lord Brown of Eaton-under-Heywood
5 Lord Scott of Foscote	11 Lord Mance
6 Lord Rodger of Earlsferry	12 Lord Neuberger of Abbotsbury

Although these 12 former Law Lords will remain members of the upper House, they will be barred from sitting and voting in the legislature for as long as they remain Justices of the Supreme Court. Those appointed subsequently, to fill vacancies arising from death or retirement, will not be made members of the House of Lords.

The qualifications for office, as set out in the CRA, remain largely as they were for the appointment of Law Lords. To be considered for appointment as a Justice of the Supreme Court, candidates must:
• have held high judicial office for at least 2 years, or
• have been a qualifying practitioner for a period of 15 years

Qualifying practitioners are those who:
• have a Senior Courts qualification
• are advocates in Scotland or solicitors entitled to appear in the Scottish Court of Session and the High Court of Justiciary, or
• are a member of the Bar of Northern Ireland or a solicitor of the Court of Judicature of Northern Ireland

Qualifications aside, however, vacancies in the court will be filled by means of an appointment process (see Box 6.3), totally unlike the mishmash of 'secret soundings' and private recommendations commonly associated with the appointment of Law Lords.

Box 6.3 The Supreme Court appointment process

1 A vacancy arises.

2 A five-member selection commission is convened to consider possible nominees and make a selection based on merit.

3 The commission submits a report to the Lord Chancellor naming a nominee.

4 The Lord Chancellor has three options:
– to accept the selection by notifying the prime minister
– to reject the selection, or
– to require the commission to reconsider its selection

5 Once notified, the prime minister must recommend the approved candidate to the queen.

6 The individual is appointed a Justice of the Supreme Court when the queen issues letters patent.

On the face of it, the appointment process appears straightforward. However, there are a number of points to mention. First, it is surprising that nominees for the Supreme Court will be selected not by the Judicial Appointments Commission created under the CRA, but by an ad hoc five-member selection commission assembled in the event of a vacancy on the Court (see Box 6.4). Although the Act states that one of the five-member commission must be a member of the Judicial Appointments Commission, it is significant that the process for selecting suitable candidates for the Court is not entirely in the hands of the body given responsibility for vetting all other senior judicial appointments.

> **Box 6.4** **The composition of the selection commission**
>
> 1 The President of the Supreme Court
> 2 The Deputy President of the Supreme Court
> 3 One member of the Judicial Appointments Commission
> 4 One member of the Judicial Appointments Board for Scotland
> 5 One member of the Northern Ireland Judicial Appointments Commission

Second, the appointment process set out in the CRA is in fact much more complicated than the summary provided in Box 6.3. For example, before the selection commission can make a recommendation to the Lord Chancellor, it is required to consult senior judges outside the commission who are not willing to be considered for the vacancy, the Lord Chancellor himself, the first minister in Scotland, the Assembly first secretary in Wales, and the secretary of state for Northern Ireland.

Third, the process becomes a good deal more complicated if the Lord Chancellor opts to reject or requires reconsideration of the individual selected by the commission, as opposed to immediately notifying the prime minister of the selection (i.e. thereby approving the candidate). Where the Lord Chancellor rejects the initial selection, for example, the commission is not permitted to renominate the same individual at the second stage. However, the Lord Chancellor would then be unable to use his power of rejection against the replacement selection offered at the second stage. The commission may re-select at the second stage a candidate who has been returned for reconsideration at the first stage, but the Lord Chancellor could then use his power to reject that individual at this second stage. The Lord Chancellor is required to notify any selection made at the third stage unless he chooses to notify a selection that he had previously required to be reconsidered at stage 1 or 2 but which had not subsequently been reselected by the commission.

While even in this simplified form the process is clearly complicated, it is easy to see how the act of filling a vacancy could turn into a form of judicial ping-pong or game of chess. The commission could look to lure the Lord Chancellor into using his power to reject a candidate at stage 1, thereby leaving the way clear for an even less palatable selection to be made at stages 2 or 3 where a further rejection would be impossible. Crucially, therefore, the Lord Chancellor no longer has the power to exercise a veto in all circumstances where he might wish to do so. In addition, the CRA requires the Lord Chancellor to explain in writing any decision to reject or force reconsideration of a selection, with such a decision only allowed on the grounds that there is insufficient evidence in support of the suitability of the candidate, or that the evidence available suggested that the selection is not the best candidate on merit.

Will the creation of the Supreme Court enhance the independence of the judiciary?

The creation of the Supreme Court and its relocation to Middlesex Guildhall was clearly not done on a whim. Indeed, the Ministry of Justice has estimated that the costs associated with these changes are likely to run to £56.9 million. The arguments justifying such expense are two-fold and were set out by the Lord Chancellor in October 2006 (see Box 6.5).

Box 6.5 **Lord Falconer on judicial independence**

Currently, the final court of appeal for the UK court system is a committee of the upper legislative house. To be appointed a member of that court is to be appointed a member of the legislature. In an age when accessibility is paramount, the court is virtually invisible. It has no separate identity apart from the House of Lords.

The inappropriateness of these arrangements extends beyond the invisibility of the final court of appeal. Sometimes, members of the Appellate Committee [the Law Lords] will vote on issues which are contentious. Lord Scott spoke and voted on the Hunting Bill. Law Lords voted on the 2005 Act.

In an age when the lawyers and the legislators were close and held similar views, and when the role of the courts in holding against the government of the day was less pronounced, the idea of an invisible court of final appeal inextricably linked to the legislature was acceptable. Now it is not.

Source: adapted from Lord Falconer, 'Constitutional reform: maturity and modernisation', a speech for the University of Manchester School of Law, 20 October 2006.

First, the move will create a far more visible Supreme Court for the UK than that previously existing in the form of the House of Lords Appellate Committee. The hope, therefore, is that the new Court might develop the kind of public profile and iconic status enjoyed by its US counterpart.

Second, it is argued that moving the Law Lords out of the House of Lords and establishing a more independent appointments process will allow for a better separation of powers between the legislature, the judiciary and the executive.

This first aim can be summed up as a desire to provide transparency, thereby stimulating public interest and trust in the institution. The second — the desire to enhance judicial independence — is reflected in many of the CRA's other provisions, not least the creation of a Judicial Appointments Commission to oversee the appointment of all senior judges other than those sitting in the Supreme Court.

There is certainly every reason to believe that the changes brought about under the CRA, specifically the greater public profile and the de-politicisation of the appointments process, will create the perception that the Court is more independent, just as the absence of such features created a suspicion of political control. Although this change in perception would, in itself, be a worthwhile outcome, we will have to wait a good deal longer before we can say whether the reforms will also bring about more tangible changes in judicial independence.

Will the Supreme Court be similar to its US counterpart?

In his speech to the University of Manchester School of Law, Lord Falconer voiced his admiration for the US Supreme Court and expressed his hope that the decision to create a similar court in the UK would result in a body that would be held in equally high regard (see Box 6.6).

Box 6.6 Lord Falconer on the US Supreme Court

Earlier this month, I visited the US Supreme Court. I was struck by the quality of its proceedings, by the authority it clearly has, and by the huge interest in it and its deliberations: lines of people outside waiting to get in…the body of the Court filled to the brim with members of the public, as well as lawyers, who had managed to get in.

Democracy and the law transparently at work: justice being done, and being seen to be done. I believe that the UK Supreme Court will establish itself as a court of similar world renown.

Source: adapted from Lord Falconer, 'Constitutional reform: maturity and modernisation', a speech for the University of Manchester School of Law, 20 October 2006.

What he went on to say, however, was that the differences between the constitutional arrangements in the UK and those in the USA — not least the question of where sovereignty lies — would make it inappropriate for the UK Supreme Court to have the power to strike down primary legislation, as is the case with the US Supreme Court. In short, Lord Falconer appeared to be trying to replicate the prestige and authority of the US Supreme Court, without affording the UK body the power that underpins much of what he admires in its American namesake.

Though it is clear that the power of the UK Supreme Court will not match that of the US model, in the short term at least, it may well appear similar in other respects.

First, the decision to locate the Court in the refurbished Middlesex Guildhall will make it a more obvious focus for media and public attention. Such popular interest is likely to be enhanced by the fact that s.47 of the CRA lifts the traditional prohibition on photographs being taken inside the Court.

Second, the appointment process — specifically the interaction between the selection commission and the Lord Chancellor — is likely to lead to the kind of wrangling and hard bargaining that more often accompanies nominations to the upper echelons of the US judiciary.

Third, there will be significant similarities between the compositions of the two Courts. Justices of the UK Supreme Court, like those in the USA, will benefit from security of tenure. The UK Court will also be of a similar size to the US model (12 Justices compared to 9), and there will be a 'Chief Justice' of sorts, in the form of the President of the Court.

Such perceived similarities and the inevitable media attention surrounding the new Court should mean that, regardless of its actual powers, the UK Supreme Court will indeed become a major force in the UK political arena.

Conclusions

We wrote our original chapter on the CRA less than 6 months after the Bill had passed into statute (see *Annual Survey 2006*, Chapter 12). At that time, we identified a number of apparent 'unknowns' relating to precisely how the Supreme Court would operate:

1 The composition of the selection commission.
2 The question of what would happen if the Lord Chancellor refused to accept the recommendation of this commission.
3 The question of how powerful the Supreme Court could be in the absence of a codified constitution with entrenched rights.
4 Whether the creation of a UK Supreme Court would bring the senior judiciary under closer media scrutiny — would the Supreme Court Justices become public figures?

As it turns out, the first two questions are not 'unknowns', but rather 'unknown knowns', as Donald Rumsfeld would say, for the answers given in this chapter are, in large part, buried within the 315 pages of the Act itself. The third and fourth questions, however, remain as hard to answer now as they were when first posed. Although we now know where the Court will be and who will be in it, the conclusions we reached in 2006 (see Box 6.7) still offer a fair appraisal of the situation regarding whether this new body will make any real difference to the UK. Ultimately, we will just have to wait and see.

Box 6.7 Predicting the future

As has been the case with the Human Rights Act 1998 and the Freedom of Information Act 2000, it is likely that the new Supreme Court will take time to establish itself in the public consciousness. The relationship between the Court, the public, the government, and Parliament will also take time to formalise. In this respect, the UK Supreme Court may have more in common with its US counterpart than one would initially think. After all, the latter's power of judicial review was not set out explicitly in Article III of the constitution, but discovered by the Court itself in cases such as *Marbury* v *Madison* (1803). It may be that the new UK Supreme Court will have to carve out a role for itself in a similar way.

Summary

- The UK Supreme Court, established under the Constitutional Reform Act 2005, will open for business when it moves into the refurbished Middlesex Guildhall in October 2009.

- The Court will take on the roles previously performed by the 12 Law Lords who make up the Appellate Committee of the House of Lords.

- The first Justices of the Supreme Court will be the 12 Law Lords in post at the time of the move in October 2009. Thereafter, a new, more independent appointment process will be used to fill vacancies resulting from the death or resignation of existing Justices.

- The absence of an entrenched, codified constitution in the UK means that the Court will probably not take on the same pivotal role enjoyed by its US counterpart.

- That said, the Court's higher public profile means that its role might develop in ways which are, as yet, unforeseen.

Chapter 7

The Lords reform White Paper: prospects for further reform?

About this chapter

The White Paper, *The House of Lords: Reform*, published in February 2007, offered the hope that the programme of Lords reform started a decade earlier might at last be completed. As the year drew to a close, however, it became apparent that this was another false dawn: not so much 'the beginning of the end' for Lords reform, as suggested in *Annual Survey 2007*, but instead 'the end of the beginning', or something worse. By October 2007, there was the suggestion that the reform process might have already reached its end, with some apparently prepared to accept that retaining the part-reformed chamber created by the House of Lords Act 1999 might represent a kind of 'least-worst option'.

This chapter examines precisely how the momentum for reform that had built up between October 2006 and the spring of 2007 was lost thereafter, and considers what is likely to happen from this point onwards. It addresses the following questions:

- What kind of House of Lords did the White Paper envisage?
- What can we learn from the Commons' and Lords' treatment of the proposals?
- Why had the campaign for reform lost its momentum by the summer of 2007?
- Will we ever see the much-heralded 'second stage' of Lords reform?

What kind of House of Lords did the White Paper envisage?

The 2007 White Paper included most of the provisions set out in the cross-party consultation document leaked to *The Times* in October 2006 (see *Annual Survey 2007*, Chapter 7). In essence, the government was looking to create a hybrid (i.e. part-elected/part-appointed) chamber that would complement the work of the Commons, without challenging its legislative primacy (see Box 7.1). Foremost in the minds of those looking to achieve this central aim was the need to enhance the independence of the second chamber, without simply creating a copy of the Commons. This goal was achieved through a number of interconnected provisions.

The 50:50 split between elected and appointed members, allied to the requirement that all members should serve a single, lengthy, non-renewable term, was clearly designed to see the Lords retain a degree of independence and a character altogether different from that of the Commons. The decision

> **Box 7.1 Key elements of the White Paper**
>
> - The primacy of the Commons to be retained.
> - A reduced second chamber of 540 members.
> - A 50:50 split between elected and appointed peers.
> - Peers to serve long, non-renewable terms.
> - Twenty per cent of the Lords to be non-political appointments and no party to have an overall majority in the chamber.
> - Appointed peers to be selected by a new, independent Statutory Appointments Commission.
> - Elected peers to be chosen under a partially open, regional party list system.
> - A system of staggered elections, similar to that in the US Senate, with one-third of elected members being chosen at each election.
> - These elections to coincide with elections to the European Parliament, i.e. every 5 years.
>
> Source: drawn from White Paper, *The House of Lords: Reform* (Cm 7027), February 2007.

to adopt a list system in respect of those elected to the new House, the proposal for a system of staggered elections along US lines, and the rule that at least 20% of those appointed should be non-political appointees, further served to reinforce the independence of the chamber: entrenching the 'hung' status of a second chamber that had existed, de facto, since the removal of most of the hereditary peers in 1999.

The White Paper left some interesting questions unanswered, for example, the issue of whether those appointed to the new House would enjoy the same public confidence as those elected directly under the partially open regional lists. That said, the provisions outlined eased the fears of some of those worried that a second chamber composed along similar lines to the Commons might serve to either:

- afford the Lords its own mandate, thereby undermining the primacy of the Commons, or
- make it less likely that the new House would be able to scrutinise the Commons effectively

In short, the publication of the White Paper in February 2007 appeared to have addressed many of the questions that had resulted from the failure of earlier reform initiatives.

What can we learn from the Commons' and Lords' treatment of the proposals?

Despite unprecedented optimism at the time when the White Paper was published, the degree of consensus that appeared to be present early in 2007 was reflected neither in the parliamentary debates surrounding the government's proposals, held in March 2007, nor in the Commons and Lords votes which followed (see Table 7.1).

Option	House of Commons			House of Lords		
	Yes	No	Majority	Yes	No	Majority
Abolition	163	416	−253	No vote taken		
100% appointed	196	375	−179	361	121	+240
50% elected	155	418	−263	46	410	−364
60% elected	178	392	−214	45	393	−348
80% elected	305	267	+38	114	336	−222
100% elected	337	224	+113	122	326	−204

Source: adapted from Meg Russell, 'The House of Lords — reform past and present', *Politics Review*, Vol. 17, No.1, September 2007.

Table 7.1 Parliamentary votes on Lords reform, March 2007

Many of the concerns and anxieties that had been raised at the time of the series of failed votes in 2003 resurfaced during more than 11 hours of Commons debate spanning 2 days. Concerns over the perceived threat to the Commons' primacy — in spite of explicit guarantees that the status quo would be preserved — and fears relating to the practicalities of reform (e.g. over the election and appointment processes and what should happen to existing peers) were central to many of the 40 or so speeches made by MPs.

What is clear is that the subtleties of these debates are not made immediately apparent from an examination of the voting figures alone. For example, though we know that 196 MPs voted in favour of an entirely appointed second chamber, their motivations for doing so are far from clear: did they value the political independence and integrity of a House free from the pressure of having to be returned via the ballot box, or were they instead fearful that an elected Lords, possessed of its own electoral mandate, would threaten the Commons' legislative primacy? Similarly, the option that won the greatest support among MPs — that of a fully elected second chamber — was not, in reality, the most popular, as many of those who filed through the lobby in support of this model did so as a wrecking tactic designed to embarrass the government and provoke conflict with the Lords over the proposed reforms.

In contrast to the surprise that greeted the outcome in the Commons (see Box 7.2), the Lords reaction to the proposals — rejecting all options bar the retention of a fully appointed House — was widely anticipated. As Jack Straw had remarked ahead of the Lords votes: 'I don't know what the bookies are offering, but the odds will be very short on the peers backing an all-appointed chamber, and long on any alternative' (*Guardian*, 6 March 2007).

Box 7.2
A surprise in the Commons

MPs excoriated government plans for a hybrid House last night as they delivered an emphatic vote in favour of a Lords that is completely elected. After more than 40 speeches and 11 hours of debate over 2 days, MPs flatly rejected Mr Straw's plan for a 50% elected element.

Source: adapted from Will Woodward, 'MPs spurn Straw's hybrid plan and deliver resounding vote for a fully elected Lords', *Guardian*, 8 March 2007.

Why had the campaign for reform lost its momentum by the summer of 2007?

As discussed in *Annual Survey 2007*, the momentum for reform that built up during 2006 was based on three interconnected factors:

- the sense that reform of the upper chamber was 'unfinished business' (see Box 7.3)
- the furore over the 'cash for peerages' affair
- the fact that many of the transitional arrangements were regarded as wholly risible, e.g. the 'elections' to the Lords that take place each time one of the remaining hereditary peers dies, or the failed 'people's peers' initiative

Box 7.3
Time to finish the job?

Nothing has become more symbolic of the Blair government's failure than the fate of its flagship constitutional reform. Nine years down the track, the Lords is stuck in a siding, after half-baked changes that settled nothing. As with so much else this government has attempted, the purpose has been admirable, the execution lamentable.

Source: Max Hastings, 'A second chamber of time-servers and losers would be contemptible', *Guardian*, 23 October 2006.

By the end of 2007, however, all three factors had been mitigated, in part at least.

First, the desire to complete 'unfinished business' had lessened with the gradual realisation that the first phase of Lords reform had already seen the emergence of a far more assertive second chamber than had been anticipated. Some feared that further reform might result in the second chamber becoming an even more obstructive House, in spite of Jack Straw's promise that the Commons would retain its primacy. At the same time, those who had welcomed the emergence of a more effective Lords argued that a second phase of reform might actually do more harm than good. As shadow defence secretary Gerald Howarth put it: 'If it is not necessary to change, it is necessary not to change' (*Guardian*, 8 March) — put simply, 'if it ain't broke, don't fix it'.

Second, the Crown Prosecution Service's decision not to press any charges in the 'cash for peerages' affair served to undermine calls for reform of the Lords.

At the height of the scandal it had seemed almost inconceivable that the power to appoint peers would remain in the hands of the prime minister. The White Paper's proposed creation of a new independent Statutory Appointments Commission was widely seen as a damage limitation exercise: a means by which the government could control any fallout from the police investigation. The exoneration of all of those questioned during the police investigation into the scandal — and the alleged cover-up — rendered the case for a new commission somewhat less pressing.

Third, the difficulty of securing root-and-branch reform of the upper House had led some to look for something more piecemeal — a more functional, 'tidying up' exercise than that originally envisaged. Lord Steel's proposals (see Box 7.4), for example, were well received, in both the Commons and the Lords.

Box 7.4 **Tidying up the loose ends**

Lord Steel has sought support for his bill, which would tidy up the current situation by making the [current] appointments commission statutory, ending the hereditary by-elections, and allowing members to retire from the chamber.

Source: *Monitor*, September 2007.

Will we ever see the much-heralded 'second stage' of Lords reform?

By the end of 2007, the immediate prospects for further reform of the House of Lords appeared as bleak as they had done at any point following the completion of the first stage of reform in 1999. Although many would like to see further changes, there is no real consensus on the key questions of what should be done and when.

In the wake of the Lords' rejection of all but the entirely appointed second chamber model, Jack Straw appeared to accept that there would need to be a further pause for reflection and, perhaps, a further set of government proposals before any significant progress could be made (see Box 7.5). Although the then justice minister may well have been buoyed by Tory MP John Bercow's plea that he should not be 'intimidated or slowed down in any way by the reactionary, antediluvian, troglodyte forces in all parties who oppose reform' (*Guardian*, 20 July), Straw appeared more than happy to postpone any talk of further reform until after the next general election at the very earliest.

Box 7.5 **Stalled again?**

Despite the seemingly decisive vote in March for a largely or wholly elected upper House, little progress has since been made. Instead the government has announced that reform will not proceed until after the general election. Gordon

---

Brown's [*The Governance of Britain*] Green Paper gave little attention to Lords Reform, and promised no specific action...Jack Straw made it clear that there will be a further period of reflection and inter-party talks, and possibly another White Paper, before reform proceeds.

Source: *Monitor,* September 2007.

Such a reluctance to countenance further Lords reform ahead of the next general election was all the more surprising given the emphasis Gordon Brown placed on the theme of constitutional renewal in the early weeks of his premiership. *The Governance of Britain* Green Paper, which is dealt with more thoroughly in Chapter 8, was remarkably imprecise on the future course of Lords reform (see Box 7.6), particularly in light of all that had gone before. The proposals in this paper offered little more than Labour had committed themselves to in their 2001 and 2005 manifestos.

Box 7.6	In danger of becoming a backwater in the constitutional reform debate?

131 The Government remains committed to further reform of the House of Lords, to increase its legitimacy, to make it more representative and ensure that it is effective in the face of the challenges of this century.

137 The Secretary of State for Justice and Lord Chancellor will continue to lead cross-party discussions with a view to bringing forward a comprehensive package to complete House of Lords reform. The Government will develop reforms for a substantially or wholly elected second chamber and will explore how the existing powers of the chamber should apply to the reformed chamber.

138 As part of this package, the Government is committed to removing the anomaly of the remaining hereditary peers. This will be in line with the wishes of the House of Commons, which voted by a majority of 280 to remove the hereditary peers in the free votes in March 2007.

Source: Green Paper, *The Governance of Britain* (Cm 7170), July 2007.

Why was there such a lack of urgency?

Jack Straw's willingness to delay further the second stage of Lords reform can, in part, be attributed to the three factors identified previously: the increased effectiveness of the current chamber; the unravelling of the police investigation into the 'cash for peerages' affair; and the prospect of more piecemeal reforms. However, the government's position was also shaped by the fact that more extensive reforms were likely to face organised opposition in the Lords itself.

Ahead of the 2005 general election, all three major parties had committed themselves to further reform of the upper House, without detailing specifics. Jack Straw's stated hope in 2007 was that the next general election would see

the parties gaining a fresh and more clearly defined electoral mandate concerning the precise form that any reformed chamber might take (see Box 7.7). Under the Salisbury Convention, such a mandate would make it hard for the Lords to block further reform. It would also make it easier for the government to justify the use of the Parliament Act, to force through reform, should the Lords fail to observe the convention.

Box 7.7	Seeking a clear mandate

The Justice Secretary, Jack Straw, yesterday put Lords reform on ice until after the next General Election, saying the best way to make progress was to secure clear manifesto commitments to a mainly elected upper House from all three main parties. Such a cross-party agreement would make it possible constitution-ally for the Commons to force through the change on the basis that the current Lords could not override the manifesto commitments of all three parties.

Source: adapted from Patrick Wintour, 'Straw delays Lords reform until after general election', *Guardian*, 20 July 2007.

Conclusions

Further reform of the House of Lords appeared a far more distant possibility at the end of 2007, than it did a year earlier. Although such sea changes are not uncommon in the field of politics, the failure of the most recent proposals is all the more surprising given the optimism with which they were received when the government published the White Paper in February.

Jack Straw's confirmation that further progress will not be possible ahead of the next general election — taken alongside Gordon Brown's announcement that such an election may not now take place until 2009 — makes it all the more likely that the *Annual Survey 2009* will be an entirely 'Lords reform-free zone'.

Summary

- The 2007 White Paper on Lords reform included many of the measures set out in the cross-party consultation document leaked to *The Times* in October 2006 (see *Annual Survey 2007*, Chapter 7):
  - the House of Commons to retain its primacy over legislation
  - an upper chamber split 50:50 between elected and appointed members who would serve a single, fixed term, far longer than that enjoyed by those in the Commons
  - elections to be held under a partially open, regional list system and staggered in three cohorts, along the same lines as the US Senate
  - appointments to be made by a new, independent Statutory Appointments Commission, with 20% of those chosen being non-political appointees

- a chamber where no single party would be allowed to enjoy an overall majority
- The Commons voted by a majority of 113 in favour of an entirely elected second chamber. Some MPs clearly backed this model of composition as a wrecking tactic designed to antagonise the Lords.
- The Lords rejected all of the proposed models apart from the one under which the second chamber would remain entirely appointed.
- The resulting impasse, taken alongside a number of contextual factors (e.g. the end of the 'cash for peerages' investigation), prompted the government to postpone further reform until after the next general election.

Chapter 8

The Governance of Britain Green Paper: a new constitutional settlement for the UK?

About this chapter

The start of Gordon Brown's tenure as prime minister was marked by the publication of a Green Paper entitled *The Governance of Britain* (Cm 7170, July 2007). Widely hailed as Brown's blueprint for a new wave of constitutional reform, the release of this document appeared to bring Labour full circle. A decade earlier, the party had come to power offering a far-reaching programme of constitutional reform comprising devolution, Lords reform, the promise of a Human Rights Act and a Freedom of Information Act, and the prospect of reform of the electoral system used in UK general elections.

Although New Labour had delivered on many of these promises, by 2007 there was the perception that in many areas the reforms were incomplete (e.g. Lords reform) or watered down (e.g. the Freedom of Information Act). This chapter examines the extent to which the 2007 Green Paper represented a genuine attempt to get the constitutional reform programme back on track. It also considers issues such as:

- whether the Green Paper offered the prospect of a less powerful, more accountable executive
- what the proposals for 're-invigorating our democracy' would mean for the UK
- whether the proposals relating to the notion of citizenship would offer anything new

Will the Green Paper help to guard against an overpowerful executive?

The first two sections of the Green Paper — 'Limiting the powers of the executive' and 'Making the executive more accountable' — were widely seen as a response to the view that the power of the executive and that of the prime minister has expanded in recent years.

Section 1 (see Box 8.1) included a number of interesting provisions relating to the exercise of prerogative powers and the management of the executive more generally. Of these proposals, the suggestion that the prime minister might lose the ability to deploy troops abroad and enter the UK into international treaties was most likely to capture the imagination of the headline writers. Although under no legal obligation to do so, recent prime ministers have often chosen to allow the legislature to vote on such issues as a means of legitimising their chosen course of action. John Major, for example, sought parliamentary approval for the Maastricht Treaty, and Tony Blair eventually allowed a Commons vote on the decision to go to war in Iraq. It was the furore over the Iraq decision (specifically the claims about weapons of mass destruction) that had helped to garner Commons' support, which brought the issue of war powers to the fore.

Box 8.1 Limiting the powers of the executive

The Government will seek to surrender or limit powers which it considers should not, in a modern democracy, be exercised exclusively by the executive...These include powers to:

- deploy troops abroad;
- request the dissolution of Parliament;
- request the recall of Parliament;
- ratify international treaties without decision by Parliament;
- determine the rules governing entitlement to passports and for the granting of pardons;
- restrict parliamentary oversight of the intelligence services;
- choose bishops;
- have a say in the appointment of judges;
- direct prosecutors in individual criminal cases; and
- establish the rules governing the Civil Service.

The Government will also:

- work to increase parliamentary scrutiny of some public appointments, ensure that appointments are appropriately scrutinised more generally; and
- review the role of the Attorney General to ensure that the office retains the public's confidence.

Source: Green Paper, *The Governance of Britain* (Cm 7170), July 2007.

In a similar vein, it was the Attorney General's 'evolving' advice on the legality of military action in Iraq ahead of the deployment of UK troops (see Box 8.2) that ultimately prompted the Green Paper's suggestion that there was a need for a 'review [of] the role of the Attorney General to ensure that the office retains the public's confidence'.

In truth, few of the proposals included in section 1 of the Green Paper were entirely new. The Liberal Democrats had included a promise of a formal War Powers Act in their 2005 general election manifesto. They had also called for a Civil Service Act designed to limit the use of the prime minister's prerogative powers to control the operation of, and appointments to, the

Box 8.2 **The Attorney General under scrutiny**

On 7 March 2003, Lord Goldsmith, the Attorney General, told Tony Blair that a second UN resolution was the safest legal option. Ten days later Lord Goldsmith's final advice was published, but included no concerns about the legality of the war. The advice of 7 March was never shown to the Cabinet — they were only given the 17 March advice. The latter advice was also made public in an answer in the House of Lords. The war started on 20 March.

Source: adapted from 'Iraq war legal advice published', BBC News website, 28 April 2005.

civil service; the suggestion being that the service had become overly politicised during the 1980s and 1990s. As was the case with the Liberal Democrats' proposals for controls on war powers, their call for civil service reform was also echoed in the Green Paper's promise of a revised ministerial code, a new set of rules governing the service, and better scrutiny of some public appointments.

The suggestion that the prime minister should lose his or her role in appointing Church of England bishops had also been long-anticipated. Margaret Thatcher's use of this power had caused considerable controversy in the 1980s (see Box 8.3), and Tony Blair's appointments to the Church were similarly controversial; not least because he regularly attended mass with his Roman Catholic wife Cherie Booth. Indeed, on leaving office, Blair announced his intention to convert to Catholicism.

Box 8.3 **Appointing bishops**

It is argued that the ability for the Prime Minister to pick one of two candidates to put forward for appointment by the Queen allows the possibility of active involvement of a Prime Minister…Professor Bogdanor gives examples…where it has been suggested that advice was given by the Prime Minister on political rather than ecclesiastical grounds:

'…on three occasions Margaret Thatcher overrode the wishes of the church and appointed the name that was second amongst the preferences of the church…in 1981 when she recommended Graham Leonard rather than John Habgood as Bishop of London, in 1987, when she recommended Mark Santer rather than Jim Thompson as Bishop of Birmingham, and in 1990, when she recommended George Carey rather than John Habgood as Archbishop of Canterbury…'

Source: Lucinda Meer, *Prime Ministerial involvement in ecclesiastical appointments*, House of Commons Library (SN/PC/4403), 24 July 2007.

As was the case with the proposed limitations on the prime minister's use of prerogative powers, the proposals designed to make the executive more accountable (see Box 8.4) could also be seen to have grown out of the experience of New Labour's first decade in government. For example:

- The stated desire to provide more transparency with regards to security policy has clearly come in response to the criticisms levelled at the government and the security services post-9/11.
- The changes to the way in which the government announces expenditure could be seen as a move aimed at placating those who have accused the government of misleading the public, by announcing individual increases in spending several times over.
- The proposed limitation on the pre-release of official statistics addresses criticisms that ministers have been able to mitigate damaging stories by virtue of the fact that they can see them coming a lot earlier than those opposition MPs shadowing them.

Box 8.4 **Enhancing the accountability of the executive**

The Government will:

- consider legislation with the aim of maximising the effectiveness of the Intelligence and Security Committee and, in the interim, propose changes to improve the transparency and resourcing of the Committee;
- publish a National Security Strategy which will be overseen by a new National Security Committee, chaired by the Prime Minister;
- introduce a pre-Queen's Speech consultative process on its legislative programme;
- simplify the reporting of Government expenditure to Parliament;
- invite Parliament to hold annual parliamentary debates on the objectives and plans of major Government Departments; and
- limit the pre-release of official statistics to Ministers to 24 hours before publication.

Source: Green Paper, *The Governance of Britain* (Cm 7170), July 2007.

What would the proposals for 're-invigorating our democracy' mean for the UK?

Section 3 of the Green Paper, entitled 'Re-invigorating our democracy', appeared to offer a number of important proposals. In reality, however, there was little of worth that was genuinely new.

Lords reform

The proposal to 'continue to develop reforms for a substantially or wholly elected second chamber' offered little more than was promised in Labour's 2005 general election manifesto. Indeed, as discussed in Chapter 7, the government has already admitted that there is unlikely to be further progress on Lords reform ahead of the next general election.

Electoral reform

The commitment to 'complete and publish a review of voting systems in line with the Government's manifesto commitment' means that electoral reform is another area in which the government appears to have made little if any progress since 2001 (see Table 8.1).

Labour's 2001 manifesto	Labour's 2005 manifesto	The Governance of Britain Green Paper, 2007
'We will review the experience of the new systems and the Jenkins report to assess whether changes might be made to the electoral system for the House of Commons. A referendum remains the right way to agree any change for Westminster.'	'Labour remains committed to reviewing the experience of the new electoral systems — introduced for the devolved administrations, the European Parliament and the London Assembly. A referendum remains the right way to agree any change for Westminster.'	'The Government will complete and publish a review of [new] voting systems in line with the Government's manifesto commitment'.

Table 8.1 'Spot the difference': Labour on electoral reform, 2001–07

All-women shortlists

The Green Paper suggested that the government might 'consider extending the duration in which parties can use all-women shortlists for the selection of electoral candidates'. New Labour employed such shortlists between 1993 and 1996, as a means of increasing the number of female MPs in the Commons. In the 1992 general election, only 10% (60) of those MPs returned were women, whereas in 1997, the figure had risen to 18% (120), the new intake commonly referred to — somewhat dismissively — as 'Blair's babes'.

Though the practice of employing such shortlists was subsequently declared illegal under the Sex Discrimination Act 1975, it was allowed once more following the Sex Discrimination (Election Candidates) Act 2002. Significantly, however, this legislation was designed not as a permanent measure but as a means of correcting historic inequalities; the result being that the Act was only set to run until 2015. It is the desirability of such a 'cut-off' which the Green Paper seeks to address.

Elections at the weekend

Recent years have seen the government innovating in a number of areas as a means of addressing historically low levels of electoral turnout; most notably the extension of postal voting and experiments with internet and SMS text voting. The Green Paper raises the possibility of the UK 'moving voting to weekends for general and local elections'. Some argue that moving the polling day to Saturday, when the majority of people are not at work, would result in increased turnout. There is no guarantee, however, that this would be the case. Although not at work, significant numbers of individuals may well be away from their homes at weekends. We should also remember that voting rates are no higher in the USA, where Election Day is a public holiday. It is significant that the government's focus appears, once again, to be on removing perceived *practical* barriers to individuals voting rather than addressing the extent to which the problem may in fact be rooted in *attitudes*.

Limiting protest outside Parliament

There is little doubt that recent decades have seen government ministers and many on the backbenches becoming less comfortable with the right to protest around the Palace of Westminster. Mass demonstrations — particularly those opposing the ban on fox hunting and the UK involvement in Iraq — have made it difficult for the security services to manage the safety of those inside Parliament effectively. Individual protests have also become more noisome to many MPs. The disruption caused by members of the group Fathers4Justice, who climbed onto the roof of Parliament, was significant. Brian Haw's 'peace camp' in Parliament Square between 2001 and 2007 and, more significantly the commotion it caused, was also regarded as both unsightly and unhelpful by many MPs.

Despite this, the effort to regulate such protests by means of the 2005 Serious Organised Crime and Police Act (SOCPA) has been met with derision and despair in equal measure. Those seeking to explore the 'funny side' of this legislation should look at the kinds of comedy 'mass lone demos' organised by comedian and activist Mark Thomas (see **www.markthomasinfo.com**). At the heart of such comedy is a serious point, however: the clear and present threat to our democratic right to protest. The Green Paper promised that the government will consult widely on the scope of SOCPA and ensure that 'people's right to protest is not subject to unnecessary restrictions'.

In addition to the headline provisions in section 3, the Green Paper also aimed to enhance further democracy at the local level — by requiring public bodies to involve local people in major decisions, by allowing local communities the chance to take control of devolved budgets and by providing better local accountability. It also sought to review and modernise the way in which the government receives and deals with petitions.

Do the proposals relating to the citizen and the state offer anything new?

There is little that is original in section 4 of the Green Paper ('Britain's future: the citizen and the state' — see Box 8.5). The long-standing debate over how best to promulgate 'British values' — brought into sharp focus by the home-grown terrorist attacks of 7/7 — surfaced once more, as did the notion of citizenship and citizenship education. The latter had originally been one of the 'cross-curricular themes' identified in the Conservatives' 1988 Education Reform Act. After 2002, it became a compulsory 'subject' for all KS3 and KS4 students.

Box 8.5 Britain's future: the citizen and the state

The Government will:

- initiate an inclusive process of national debate to develop a British statement of values;
- work with Lord Goldsmith to conduct a review of British citizenship;
- launch a Youth Citizenship Commission, looking at citizenship education, ceremonies and the possibility of reducing the voting age; and
- consult on the current guidance on flying the Union Flag from government buildings and Westminster Parliament.

Source: Green Paper, *The Governance of Britain* (Cm 7170), July 2007

The suggestion that the voting age could be reduced from 18 to 16 — another proposal widely discussed in recent years — was criticised by the Constitution Unit. 'Lowering the voting age to 16 would almost certainly reduce voter turnout,' it argued, and '18–25 year olds already vote less than older age groups, and the risk is that young voters who start in life not voting are likely to continue as non-voters.'

When and where should we fly the flag?

One element of the Green Paper that had certainly not been anticipated was the offer of consultation 'on the current guidance on flying the Union Flag from government buildings and Westminster Parliament'. Though the flying of the Union flag — indeed most flags — has long been a source of political controversy in Northern Ireland, the issue has rarely made it onto the political agenda in England. While the proposals may indeed have merit, therefore, it is hard to escape the conclusion that the 500 or so words devoted to the subject in the Green Paper — or time spent producing the eight-page flag-flying consultation document published subsequently (see Box 8.6) — could not have been more usefully employed addressing some more pressing topic.

Box 8.6 The burning issue of the twenty-first century?

Currently Government buildings only fly the Union Flag on the 16 flag flying days specified by the Department for Media, Culture and Sport (DCMS).

The Green Paper stresses the importance of the Union Flag to national identity and introduces the possibility of wider flag flying on Government buildings following a consultation process.

James Purnell, the Secretary of State for Culture, decided on Thursday, 5 July 2007 to give UK government department buildings in England, Scotland and Wales the freedom to fly the Union Flag at all times, whilst this consultation process is underway.

Source: adapted from *Consultation on altering the current guidance on flying the Union Flag from UK Government buildings*, DCMS, July 2007.

Ironically, perhaps, it is a proposal not headlined in the Executive Summary of section 4 of the Green Paper, but included in the detail, that might prove the most significant. That is the suggestion that the Human Rights Act 1998 could evolve into a more formal Bill of Rights and Duties. As the Green Paper puts it:

> The Human Rights Act should not necessarily be regarded as the last word on the subject. During the Parliamentary Debates in 1997 and 1998, incorporating the Convention rights and freedoms into UK law was described as the first step in a journey…A Bill of Rights and Duties could provide explicit recognition that human rights come with responsibilities and must be exercised in a way that respects the human rights of others.

Though the problems associated with drafting such a Bill will mean that it is unlikely to come to fruition in the short term, the way in which such a document would link rights and responsibilities would certainly be in keeping with the government's emphasis on citizenship.

Conclusions

Although the 63-page *The Governance of Britain* Green Paper says a great deal, few of its provisions are truly original, and those that are, are often of questionable merit. Even groups such as the Constitution Unit, which welcomed the broad thrust of the paper, had their reservations (see Box 8.7). Moreover, only time will tell just how many of the proposals included in the document will ultimately find their way onto the statute books. New Labour's record on converting proposals into law in the area of constitutional reform has been somewhat mixed.

| Box 8.7 | 'Could do better' |

The thrust of making executive power more accountable is strongly to be welcomed, but the government could have gone further in two respects.

Firstly, while subjecting the prerogative powers to more control, the Prime Minister could give up his patronage power to select party members in the House of Lords and give his power to the House of Lords Appointments Commission.

Secondly, making the power of dissolution subject to parliamentary vote is not an effective check on abuse of the power. If the PM really wanted to restrict his power to choose the date of the next election, he should introduce fixed term parliament as Canada has just done.

Source: Constitution Unit, September 2007, adapted from *Monitor*, Issue 37.

Summary

- *The Governance of Britain* Green Paper 2007 was widely hailed in the press as a blueprint for far-reaching constitutional reform.

- It focused largely on the means by which the prime minister's use of prerogative powers could be limited — and scrutiny of the executive be further enhanced.
- The paper offered little that was genuinely new. Most of its key proposals had been trailed by one or more parties in their 2005 general election manifestos.
- The paper failed to offer firm proposals in a number of key areas (e.g. Lords reform).
- The suggestion that the Human Rights Act could develop into a formal Bill of Rights and Duties was significant, but the proposal was heavily qualified and not made subject to any timescale.
- It remains to be seen just how many, if any, of the Green Paper's proposals find their way onto the statute books ahead of the next general election.

Chapter 9

The end of Ming: where now for the Liberal Democrats?

About this chapter

Less than 2 years after ousting Charles Kennedy, the Liberal Democrats instigated another leadership contest in 2007. This chapter examines why Sir Menzies Campbell was toppled, the impact of his brief leadership and the ensuing contest between Nick Clegg and Chris Huhne.

Why was Campbell doomed?

By the autumn of 2007, there was growing unease among Liberal Democrats; their annual conference in September was described by one journalist as 'a gathering of the deflated, depressed and disgruntled' (*Daily Telegraph*, 18 September 2007). This unease was sparked mainly by the party's lack of progress among voters, of which there had been ample evidence throughout 2007:

- In the English council elections, they lost control of 11 councils and suffered a net loss of 257 seats.
- In the Scottish Parliament and Welsh Assembly elections, the party again faltered, capturing less than 14% of votes. In Scotland, the party also found itself out of power for the first time, its 8-year coalition with Labour making way for a minority SNP administration.
- Opinion polls showed Liberal Democrat support steadily dropping; by September it was as low as 11%. In other words, the party appeared to have lost half its support since the 2005 general election.

These figures inevitably drew attention to Sir Menzies Campbell, who had taken over as leader following the dethronement of Charles Kennedy in January 2006. Three particular criticisms were levelled by those inside (and outside) the party:

- Following the advent of David Cameron, and a new 'liberal Conservatism', Campbell had failed to develop a new Liberal Democrat strategy to impress volatile centre-right voters. As such, there was clear evidence that former Liberal Democrat voters in southern England were now drifting towards the Tories (exemplified by the loss of Torbay and Bournemouth in the May council elections).
- Campbell had hesitated before rejecting Gordon Brown's invitation (in May) to join a 'government of all the talents', involving several Liberal Democrat cabinet ministers. The outcome of Campbell's response was said to be:

– an impression of weak leadership
– an impression that Liberal Democrats were no longer 'equidistant' between the main two parties, but significantly closer to Labour — not encouraging for those tired of Labour rule. With Brown's offer rejected, it seemed that Campbell had left the party with the 'worst of all worlds': still not a party of power, yet now discredited as a party of opposition.

- In a culture that prized youthful zest, Campbell (aged 66) was seen as too old to entice new voters (the comparison with Cameron was stark). As one Liberal Democrat MP put it: 'Party leaders today are judged less by their cool judgement than by their 'hottie' rating on Facebook.' Moreover, his patrician style often evoked the politics of a by-gone age, with another MP describing him as 'looking more like the heir to Gladstone than Brown' (*Daily Telegraph*, 17 October 2007). Campbell's problems in this respect were compounded by a less than relaxed manner on television.

How important was the 2007 Liberal Democrat conference?

During the party's conference, there was intense rumour and speculation about Campbell's future. This was fuelled by MPs Nick Clegg and Chris Huhne who told fringe meetings they would be 'interested' in the leadership should a vacancy arise, and Lord Rodgers (former party leader in the Lords) who claimed that Campbell's record was 'disappointing'.

Aware that his leadership was in peril, Campbell unveiled what he hoped would be exciting policy initiatives, notably tax reforms that would 'shift the burden from the many to the few'. However, given his admission that households earning over £70,000 per annum 'would and should pay more', these ideas did little to rescue flagging Liberal support among southern, suburban voters. Indeed, they may have contributed to the Tories' surge in support a fortnight later.

However, the development that sealed Campbell's fate came a week after the conference, when Gordon Brown announced that there would not, after all, be an autumn general election. For many Liberal Democrats, this removed the only reason for not dumping Campbell sooner rather than later.

How was Campbell toppled?

If the overthrow of Kennedy was prolonged and tortuous (see *Annual Survey 2007*), that of Campbell was swift and ruthless:

- On 12 October, the *Daily Telegraph* reported a senior Liberal Democrat MP saying of Campbell: 'He will be gone by Christmas…there is no support for him in the grassroots.'

- On 13 October, party president Simon Hughes told ITV that Campbell 'must do better' at getting the party's message across.
- On 14 October, the party's Treasury spokesman, Vincent Cable, admitted that the leadership was 'under discussion'.
- On 15 October, at 6.30 p.m., Campbell resigned, explaining: 'It has become clear that, following the prime minister's decision not to hold an election, questions about leadership are getting in the way of further progress by the party.'

Was Campbell underrated?

Amid the reasons given for his downfall, it should be recalled that Campbell's reign as leader had some positive aspects:
- He oversaw extensive modernisation of the party's headquarters and its organisation outside Parliament.
- He fast-tracked some of the party's brightest, younger MPs, including Clegg and Huhne.
- He oversaw certain policy initiatives that pre-empted those of other parties, particularly in relation to the environment and inheritance tax.
- He presided over some creditable performances in the elections of 2006–07. In by-elections, Liberal Democrats took the safe Labour seat of Dunfermline West, and almost took the safe Tory seat of Bromley and Chislehurst (see *Annual Survey 2007*). In the English council elections, the party still managed roughly a quarter of votes cast — consistent with its score under previous Liberal Democrat leaders.

The 2007 leadership contest: who were the contenders?

By the close of nominations, only two contenders for the leadership had emerged: home affairs spokesman Nick Clegg (securing nominations from 22 Liberal Democrat MPs) and environment spokesman Chris Huhne (with 12 nominations). Box 9.1 contains a brief biography of both contenders.

Box 9.1	Liberal Democrat leadership candidates 2007

Nick Clegg
Aged 38, charismatic and telegenic — 'looking and sounding like Blair and Cameron rolled into one' (*Daily Telegraph*, 16 October 2007) — Clegg has long been spoken of as a future party leader. He was educated at Westminster and Cambridge, and was an MEP before becoming MP for Sheffield Hallam in 2005. Identified with the centre-right, 'Orange Book' wing of the party, his campaign sought to link the party to economic liberalism as well as social liberalism, allying support for lower tax and privatisation to endorsements of gay marriage, sexual equality and vigorous anti-racism. His campaign also attacked compulsory ID cards and defended Britain's independent nuclear deterrent.

Chris Huhne

Aged 53, Huhne came a creditable second in the leadership race of 2006 and then cultivated a solid base of grass-roots supporters. Educated at Westminster and Oxford, he was a journalist and businessman before becoming MP for Eastleigh in 2005. His appointment as environment spokesman reflected his long-standing interest in the subject and the tone of his 2006 leadership bid. In his 2007 campaign, he was again keen to emphasise the party's commitment to a 'green' agenda and defended Campbell's idea of higher tax for the highest income groups. In his campaign, he called for the unilateral scrapping of Britain's nuclear deterrent and supported Tory plans to exclude Scottish MPs from votes on English laws.

The result

Around 64,000 ballot papers were distributed to Liberal Democrat members across the country, with all votes carrying equal weight. The result was declared on 18 December:

Box 9.2   2007 Liberal Democrat leadership contest: the result

Nick Clegg: 20,988 (50.6%)

Chris Huhne: 20,477 (49.4%)

Turnout (approx.): 65%

Conclusion

The result was rather different to the one envisaged by most commentators at the start of the campaign: what was once thought to be a 'shoo-in' for Clegg turned out to be the narrowest of victories — and one that gave the new leader a rather precarious basis for his new regime. It was reported that Clegg had haemorrhaged considerable support during the campaign, as many members were dismayed by his cautious approach to Europe, his fondness for free-market economics, his indifference to electoral reform and his striking similarity (in terms of style, looks and rhetoric) to the Tory leader, David Cameron.

In the aftermath of the result, some observers were claiming that a Clegg–Cameron axis might develop in the years ahead, heightening the possibility of a Lib-Con pact — even coalition — in the event of a hung parliament. However, as the leadership result indicates, Clegg may find it hard to lead his party in such a centre-right direction. As such, the strategy of Britain's third party remained uncertain at the close of 2007.

Chapter 10

The funding of political parties: could Phillips make a difference?

About this chapter

In the *Annual Survey 2007*, we examined the 'problem' of party finance and the various attempts to solve it. It was observed that all the main parties had cash-flow problems, while their sources of income (particularly loans and donations from institutions and wealthy individuals) only seemed to compound the parties' unpopularity. This chapter looks at two official responses to the issue of party funding — the report of Sir Hayden Phillips and the report of the Constitutional Affairs Select Committee — and considers the significance of their findings. In doing so, the chapter focuses on questions such as:

- Why do the sources of party revenue remain contentious?
- How and why do the Conservative, Labour and Liberal Democrat parties differ on party funding?
- Why are the Phillips recommendations 'vague and inconclusive'?
- Does the lack of consensus between the parties on the Phillips proposals mean that party funding will remain 'a problematic and divisive issue'?

What were the main contributions to the debate about party funding?

Between December 2006 and March 2007, two authoritative reports appeared in relation to the financing of political parties:

- *Party Funding*, a report by the Constitutional Affairs Select Committee, released in December 2006 (although important, this report was over-shadowed by the second major contribution to the debate).
- *Strengthening Democracy: Fair and Sustainable Funding of Political Parties*, a report released in March 2007 following a review chaired by Sir Hayden Phillips.

The Constitutional Affairs Select Committee report

The Select Committee's report served a useful purpose by uncovering and high-lighting crucial figures for students of party finance. It pointed out, for example, that the British taxpayer was already subsidising British parties to a substantial extent (see Box 10.1). It also showed that:

- During the previous 5 years, 64% of Labour's donations came from trade unions. This finding refuted Jack Straw's claim in 2006 that union donations

now accounted for just 26% of party income. Labour is therefore more reliant on unions than some of its spokespeople care to admit.

- Twenty-nine trade unions had political funds; 17 of them donated such funds to the Labour Party.
- The Tories received a much broader range of donations than other parties, with donations of over £100,000 representing 43% of party income.

Box 10.1 **State subsidies to political parties: some recent examples**

- In 2006–07, the three main parties each received almost £456,000 from the state's Policy Development Fund (set up by the Political Parties, Elections and Referendums Act 2000).

- At Westminster, opposition parties in 2006–07 received over £6 million of 'short money' (designed to help meet the cost of their administration and other parliamentary business).

- During 2006–07, the parties' television election broadcasts received subsidies worth £16 million (having been £68 million during the general election year of 2005).

- At the 2005 general election, the parties' postal costs were met by a grant of £20 million.

What did the Select Committee recommend?

The Select Committee had taken a close look at the funding of parties in Canada, Germany and the USA. It also undertook a critical reassessment of the Neill Report (1998) into party funding and the subsequent Political Parties, Elections and Referendums Act 2000, which revised the rules for state assistance, donations and campaign spending. According to the Select Committee, the Act's measures had been less than comprehensive and its loopholes had come to light during the 'raising and spending' controversies of 2006 (see *Annual Survey 2007*). It therefore recommended that:

- National campaign spending levels in a general election should be reduced from the £20 million maximum created by the 2000 Act — it did not recommend a new figure.
- Spending should be capped over a 5-year period — thus taking account of other election campaigns and the 'ongoing' campaign in marginal seats between elections.
- The main parties should agree among themselves a figure that caps both individual and institutional donations
- State aid to parties should be extended, but in a way that reflects arrangements in Canada. Funds would therefore be directed more at local party organisations and allocated in a way that rewarded the recruitment of new members.

The Select Committee's report received a favourable response from many Labour backbenchers and opposition MPs. The government, however, chose not to respond until the publication of the Phillips Report, as Sir Hayden had indicated he would take account of the Select Committee's proposals.

The Phillips Report

What were its origins?

Prime Minister Blair commissioned the Phillips inquiry in March 2006, as a response to growing concerns about party finance, particularly the 'loans for lordships' allegations behind the arrest of Lord Levy, one of Labour's principal fundraisers. It was billed by Blair as 'the most comprehensive analysis of party funding for over 30 years' — a reference to the Houghton Report, commissioned by a previous Labour government in 1975.

Who had input?

According to Sir Hayden, his team received almost 2,000 letters and e-mails from members of the public in addition to a 'lively and informative' exchange during a 'question-and-answer webchat'. However, given Phillips's wish to achieve cross-party consensus, the most influential contributions came from the parties themselves.

Conservatives

The Conservatives had argued for:
- a £50,000 cap on donations
- a reduction in the legal limit for national campaign spending to £15 million
- additional state funding based on party performance at the previous general election
- an end to all corporate and institutional donations

It was argued that the Tories were being disingenuous in respect of donations. While it was known that Labour was heavily reliant on a small number of donations that far exceeded £50,000, the Tories received many smaller donations that usually represented about a third of their income. Furthermore, the Tories' historic links with business had always been more individual than institutional, focusing on sympathetic company chairmen and directors. So whereas an end to institutional links would cripple Labour, on account of its financial links with trade unions, it would have only limited impact on the Tories.

Nevertheless, it was significant that the Tories endorsed the principal of capping donations, which they had hitherto opposed, and quite startling that they conceded the case for further state assistance. This was something they had resisted historically and which jarred with their ideological distaste for 'bailing out' loss-making outfits and any extension of the state's responsibilities.

Labour

Labour, unsurprisingly, rejected the Tories' proposal on capping. It claimed that any severance of its financial links with the unions marked an attack on the history and character of the Labour movement (the party having been effectively founded by the unions in 1900). Labour argued that the issue of donations was less important than reducing the limit on campaign expenditure, *both during and between general elections* (an indication that Labour was worried about the Tories' policy of targeting marginal seats over a 3–4 year period). If there were a stricter cap on what the parties could spend, Labour argued, there would be less concern about how the parties' money was raised.

Liberal Democrats

The Liberal Democrats echoed the Tories' call for a cap on donations and Labour's wish for reduced campaign expenditure. Yet their main interest was more state aid based on votes. They were particularly unhappy with the current allocation of 'short money', based mainly on seats won at a general election. As Sir Menzies Campbell pointed out, the Tories won 10% more votes than the Liberal Democrats at the 2005 general election; yet in 2006–07 they received almost three times as much short money (£4.3 million compared to the Liberal Democrats' £1.5 million). As Campbell explained, although short money was designed to meet parliamentary costs, it still relieved pressure on party funds raised outside Parliament, giving the Tories a significant advantage over the Liberal Democrats.

What did Phillips recommend?

Phillips's final report was expected in December 2006. That it did not appear until March 2007 showed that the inter-party consensus it sought was elusive. The lack of consensus also meant that, in many respects, Sir Hayden's recommendations seemed vague and inconclusive (see Box 10.2). Phillips stressed that the proposals 'could not be cherry-picked' and that 'nothing should be agreed until everything is agreed'. However, it quickly became clear that such across-the-board agreement was improbable.

Box 10.2 **Recommendations of the Phillips Report, March 2007**

Donations
Phillips accepted that the status quo was 'unsustainable' and that donations to parties should be limited. It went on to endorse the Conservative suggestion that a cap should be set at £50,000, but recognised that this would intrude on the historic relationship between Labour and affiliated trade unions. As a compromise, it suggested that a union's payments to Labour might be recorded as a collection of individual donations, none of which would exceed the £50,000 limit. However, Phillips acknowledged that this would present each union with stern organisational challenges which, in turn, meant extensive discussion before any reform could be implemented.

Campaign spending

Phillips argued that recent problems over donations and loans stemmed from 'excessive and unnecessary' party spending at election time. Urging the parties to adopt a more 'level-headed' and 'cost-effective' approach to spending, he recommended that each party should aim to reduce its campaign spending. Again, the report was loath to commit itself to a definite figure, but hinted at reductions of up to £20 million over a 5-year period. He also suggested that spending limits were required at constituency, as well as national, level.

State assistance

Phillips insisted that any increase in state funding should be contingent on reforms to both donations and campaign spending. If this were achieved, he argued, then up to £25 million of extra public money could be channelled into the parties, via two separate formulae:

- 'Pence per vote', linked to electoral performance. Parties would receive 50p a year for each vote won in the previous general election, and 25p each year for each vote won in the previous European and devolution elections.

- 'Pence per member', linked to member recruitment. Each new membership subscription would be matched by £5 of public funding.

How did the parties react to the Phillips proposals?

The two main opposition parties broadly welcomed the report. The then Conservative chairman Francis Maude indicated that he would be happy to limit campaign spending and thought the proposals for extra state aid 'reasonable'. However, he rejected the idea of restricting both spending between elections and at constituency level (mindful, perhaps, of the Tories marginal seats policy). David Heath, for the Liberal Democrats, applauded Sir Hayden and urged Labour to 'grasp the nettle'.

Labour flatly rejected a cap on union donations, preferring to focus instead on the limitation of localised campaign spending — an issue which Phillips had not addressed and which the Tories vigorously resisted.

Conclusion: *plus ça change?*

The lack of a consensual response to the Phillips Report meant it was effectively shelved; as Sir Hayden had always pointed out, to make a difference, his report would have to ignite a series of inter-party discussions, leading to agreement on loans, spending and state aid. The dissonance over loans (based on Labour's implacable defence of its union links) and spending (based on the Tory defence of local autonomy) made agreement over any package of reforms unlikely, thus negating the unexpected consensus over state aid. As Matthew Norman wrote in the *Independent* (16 March 2007), 'the whole exercise has been a hopeless waste of time'.

Meanwhile, in the months that followed the Phillips Report, various develop-ments showed that party finance remained a problematic and divisive issue:

- In April, the government introduced a taxpayer-funded communications allowance of £10,000 a year for MPs to spend on promoting themselves to their constituents. The government also announced that the allowance could be supplemented by up to £9,000 from MPs' staffing allowance and by the whole of their £21,339 incidental expenses provision. In short, MPs were allowed an extra £40,000 of extra public funding to spend in a way that could easily advantage them at a general election. Opposition to the reform (one Phillips did not anticipate) came from the *Guardian* and *Daily Telegraph*, which both claimed it was a further example of how political funding distorted fair electoral competition.

- The main parties remained in serious debt. In June, it was reported that:
  - the Conservatives had debts of over £16 million, despite the sale of Conservative Central Office
  - Labour continued to have reported debts of over £20 million, attracting interest rate charges of over £1.2 million a year
  - the Liberal Democrats had debts totalling £1.2 million

- The parties remained dangerously reliant on a small number of wealthy benefactors. In 2007, Labour had to find over £9 million to service the repayment of loans that sparked the 'cash for peerages crisis' (see *Annual Survey 2007*). The Tories too owed four particular benefactors, including notably Lord Ashcroft and Johan Eliasch, over £11 million. The repayment of Eliasch took on extra urgency in September after he abandoned the party in August — another reminder of how perilous 'plutocratic' funding can be.

- Despite the acquittal of Lord Levy, Labour was inevitably damaged by the 'cash for peerages' inquiry. As such, it became harder for Labour to lure support from wealthy businessmen, forcing it again to rely heavily on trade unions (whose donations in 2007 rose to 78% of Labour revenue). As Labour insiders acknowledged, this did not chime with Gordon Brown's effort to transcend 'tribal' politics.

- As talk mounted of an autumn 2007 general election, contributions to the main parties confirmed huge inequalities of income. Between February and May, Labour (buoyed by the prospect of new leadership) raised about £5 million, yet the Tories raised £6.3 million. The Liberal Democrats, meanwhile, managed a relatively meagre £1.2 million — another factor that may have led to a change of leadership at the end of the year.

- The issue of party funding may have affected the prime minister's decision to avoid an autumn general election. As indicated above, Labour's finances were in a less than robust condition and party treasurers were said to be 'extremely nervous' about fighting an election campaign (*Guardian*, 5 October 2007). In addition, surveys showed that, in crucial marginal seats, the Tories were in a much stronger position than national polls suggested —

an effect, perhaps, of Lord Ashcroft who had donated £30,000 of extra campaign funds to the party's target seats. This, in turn, made Labour MPs even keener on new limits for constituency spending — a move unlikely to produce the cross-party consensus that eluded Phillips.

- In December, it was revealed that Labour had received over £673,000 in donations from property developer David Abrahams — donations that were used to fund, among other things, the deputy leadership campaign of Harriet Harman and the Scottish leadership campaign of Wendy Alexander. It duly became clear that most of the donations were officially attributed not to Abrahams himself but to four proxy donors, something explicitly prohibited by Labour's own legislation of 2000. To compound this scandal, there were suggestions that, following Abrahams's covert largesse, some of his planning applications were fast-tracked by ministers.

As a result, 2007 closed with the links between party finance and 'sleaze' being stronger than ever, and with Labour's own funding being the source of renewed controversy (the party's General Secretary, Peter Watt, being forced to resign over the issue). Although some argued that 'donorgate' bolstered the case for further state aid, others saw it as irrefutable proof that political parties cannot be trusted with taxpayers' money. The report of Sir Hayden Phillips seems unlikely to resolve this or any of the other pressing issues surrounding party finance.

Summary

- The sources of party revenue remain contentious.
- There is limited inter-party consensus on what should be done.
- The lack of consensus hindered the Phillips review.
- The lack of consensus means the proposals contained in the Phillips Report may be futile.